The Persian Empire

*A Captivating Guide to the History of Persia,
Starting from the Ancient Achaemenid, Parthian,
and Sassanian Empires to the Safavid, Afsharid,
and Qajar Dynasties*

Free Bonus from Captivating History
(Available for a Limited time)

Hi History Lovers!

Now you have a chance to join our exclusive history list so you can get your first history ebook for free as well as discounts and a potential to get more history books for free! Simply visit the link below to join.

Captivatinghistory.com/ebook

Also, make sure to follow us on:

Twitter: @Captivhistory

Facebook: Captivating History:@captivatinghistory

Contents

INTRODUCTION 1

CHAPTER 1 – WHO ARE THE PERSIANS? THE HISTORY OF HUMAN POPULATION IN IRAN 3

CHAPTER 2 – THE BIRTH OF THE ACHAEMENID EMPIRE: THE RISE AND REIGN OF CYRUS THE GREAT 11

CHAPTER 3 – THE GLORY OF THE ACHAEMENID EMPIRE: CAMBYSES & DARIUS 20

CHAPTER 4 – THE BEGINNING OF THE END: THE REIGN OF XERXES AND THE DOWNFALL OF THE ACHAEMENID DYNASTY .. 38

CHAPTER 5 – LIFE IN ANCIENT PERSIA 57

CHAPTER 6 – THE PERSIAN MILITARY 62

CHAPTER 7 – ZOROASTRIANISM: PERSIA'S RELIGION 66

CHAPTER 8 – LATER PERSIAN DYNASTIES: THE PARTHIAN EMPIRE TO THE QAJAR DYNASTY 70

CHAPTER 9 – PERSIAN ART: MIXING EAST AND WEST 84

CHAPTER 10 – PERSIAN CONTRIBUTIONS TO SCIENCE AND TECHNOLOGY 97

CONCLUSION 102

BIBLIOGRAPHY 104

Introduction

Students of ancient history are well aware of the Persians. A still-present cultural and linguistic group, the Persians are the founders of today's modern-day nation of Iran. They trace their roots back to the Aryans of Northern Europe, but over the course of time, they managed to assert a distinct identity that led to the formation of some of the world's most powerful empires.

One of the most shocking things about the Persians is how quickly they went from an obscure, powerless, and nomadic tribe to an immense empire that spanned across western Asia, Africa, and parts of Europe. The rise of Cyrus the Great, considered the father of Persia, in the 7th century BCE filled the power vacuum caused by the fall of the Assyrians, and it led to the formation of one of the most powerful empires of the ancient world.

This first empire, known as the Achaemenid Empire, controlled one of the biggest empires by land area ever recorded. Persian troops made it as far west as Libya and Greece, and Persian governments controlled the territories in the modern-day nations of Afghanistan, Uzbekistan, and Tajikistan, as well as India. Their constant wars with the Greeks played a pivotal role in the development of this culture by forcing the Greek city-states to unite, leading to a Greek

Golden Age, which has had a tremendous influence on the world we live in today; had the Greeks been unable to stop the Persian advance, there's no telling how different the world would be.

However, like all empires of the ancient world, the Achaemenids would not last forever. Constant war depleted their resources, and the rise of the Greeks and Macedons under Alexander the Great eventually pushed the great Persian Empire into the background of history. But the Persians were not to disappear forever. Successive dynasties starting in the 3rd century BCE and continuing until the 7th century CE helped reestablish Persia as a dominant force in the region, and they played a major role in the creation and propagation of a Persian cultural and ethnic identity that would last throughout the nearly 900 years of Islamic rule and continue up until the present day.

The Persians have made significant contributions to world culture, ranging from their ability to raise and train one of the ancient world's most formidable fighting forces, the Persian Immortals, to their new and effective ways of organizing and administering government. And Persian art heavily influenced their Muslim invaders, helping to usher in the Islamic Golden Age that helped spread Islam throughout the Middle East and Africa.

Some aspects of Persian culture would disappear through time, but many would remain, even if only in small pockets. Zoroastrianism, for example, one of the world's oldest monotheistic religions, played an important role in Persian culture and identity until the Islamic invasion, but it is still around today and practiced by thousands of people across Iran and India. So, while the glory of the Persian Empire is very much a thing of the past, its influence on the world is not. As such, understanding how the Persians rose to power, and how they exerted their influence on the many different cultural groups in western Asia, helps us better understand both the history of the Middle East as well as the entire world.

Chapter 1 – Who Are the Persians? The History of Human Population in Iran

Nowadays, Persia is a household name. People eat Persian food, enjoy Persian goods, and millions of people speak the Persian language. And it has become nearly synonymous with the modern country of Iran. But this was not always the case. In fact, when examining history using a broad perspective, the Iranians are relatively new to the Middle Eastern scene. But a combination of chance, cultural development, and military might would quickly change this and turn Persia and the Persian people into one of the world's most famous civilizations. However, before looking at how the Persian Empire rose to power, it's important to understand the origins of the Persian people and also the land they would eventually call home.

The Arrival of the Iranians and the Persians

The civilization eventually understood as Persia gets its name from the region of Persis, which is located in northwestern Iran in the modern region of Fars. It is here where the Iranian tribe, the

Pasargadae, sometimes referred to as the Parsua, decided to settle in the 7th century BCE after a long and slow migration from the north and west. The city they built, also named Pasargadae, would become the cultural and political center of the early Persian Empire. However, while the modern conception of Persian civilization did not officially begin until the last millennium BCE, the story of the Persian people starts much earlier in the timeline of human history.

Evidence of human populations in Iran dates all the way back to the Late Glacial Age as well as the Late Stone Age. However, archaeological evidence suggests humans did not start abandoning their nomadic lifestyle in favor of a sedentary one based on agriculture until the 5th or perhaps even 6th century BCE.

And as people began to give up their nomadic ways in favor of sedentary, agricultural civilizations, mass migrations took place, bringing peoples from many different ethnic and linguistic backgrounds toward the Middle East. It is believed the Persians are the result of a mixing of Eastern and Western ethnicities, largely those originating from the Central Asian plateau, and also the Aryans and other ethnic groups who trace their beginnings back to Russia and many of today's Slavic states.

As was common for ancient civilizations, upon the settlement of Persis, the tribes named a leader, or king. However, this "king" would have had power only over the tribe that had granted him the right to rule, and he would have had virtually no influence over surrounding territories. This would change rather rapidly when placed within the context of ancient history (Persia would begin flexing its imperial muscles less than 200 years after the founding of Pasargadae), but in the beginning, the Persians would have been vassals to other more powerful groups in the region, specifically the Medes.

The Medes were an ethnic group and eventual kingdom (and perhaps empire, depending on how one defines the term) who were contemporaries of the Late Assyrian Empire (c. 1000 BCE-600

BCE). They are believed to have arrived onto the scene as early as the 2nd or possibly even the 3rd century BCE, and they would eventually control large parts of Northwestern Iran, Southeastern Turkey, and Western Iraq. Unfortunately, no Medes site has ever been excavated, and most of what is known about the civilization has been learned by studying the records of surrounding civilizations. So, while they were certainly influential in the region, the extent of their political control in the region is unknown, and it's believed they, generally speaking, held a loose grip on power that was largely dependent on the wills and whims of their more powerful neighbors, specifically the Elamites and the Assyrians.

However, the role of the Medes in shaping Persian history cannot be understated. While the Persians would have been subjects to this neighboring kingdom, similarities in language and religion helped bring these two peoples closer together. Specifically, the Medes and the Persians both spoke an Iranian language and are part of the Iranian ethnic group. Neither would have been able to fully understand the other, but the similarity in the structure of these two languages would have made it easier for the two groups to communicate and form networks of trade and political power.

Distinct from the Semitic languages spoken throughout much of Mesopotamia and Western Asia at the time, the Iranians are an ethnolinguistic group comprised of many different other ethnic groups, such as the Bactrians, Cimmerians, Medes, Parthians, Persians, and Scythians, among others, with the unifying characteristic of this ethnolinguistic group being the Iranian language. Iranian is a part of the broader Indo-Iranian language group, which is a branch of the much wider Indo-European classification that includes some 445 living languages, including Spanish, Hindi, English, Portuguese, Punjab, German, French, Italian, and Persian, among others.

Furthermore, at the time of Persian arrival into Iran, they were practicing a religion that would have been familiar to the Medes, for both shared their roots in the Antidemonic Law traditions known to have been a prominent part of Aryan culture (the peoples originating from Russia and other parts of northeastern Europe).

This religion had no "gods." Instead, life on Earth was understood to be controlled by a series of unnamed demons that were responsible for all the terrible things that can define existence. And they were essentially a fire cult, worshiping sacred fire as their primary deity. However, as the Persians settled and became more influential in the region, they would begin to adapt some of the religious practices of the Medes and other Iranian cultures in the region, eventually giving birth to Zoroastrianism, the largest religion to come out of Iran with the exception of Islam.

However, the Persians, with their Iranian language and Iranian/Aryan religious customs, would have been dramatically different from the other cultures already living there. When they arrived in the Fertile Crescent (the area including Mesopotamia—the large fertile valley between the Tigris and Euphrates Rivers in modern-day Iraq, as well as the surrounding territories in modern-day Israel and the Persian Gulf. See Figure 1 below.), they would have been considered "northerners." And because of their distinct language, they would have also been considered "foreigners"; at the time, most of the people in the region spoke a Semitic language, such as Assyrian, Akkadian, Babylonian, etc. This classification would play an important role in shaping the geopolitical landscape of Iran and the surrounding territory.

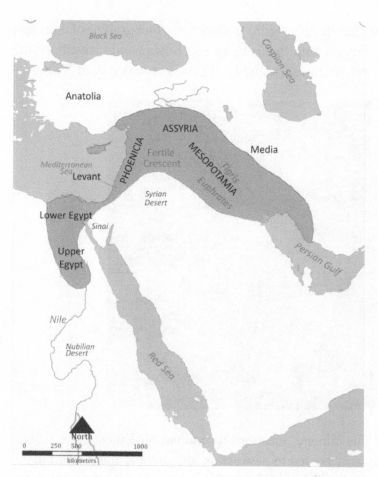

The Geography and Geopolitics of the Middle East: The Birth of the Persian Empire

Apart from the cultural, religious, and linguistic differences that existed in the ancient Middle East, the geography of the region also played a critical role in shaping the course of the region's history. The best word to describe the Iranian plateau and the surrounding territories is harsh. Mountains surround nearly the entire region. In the north, bordering the Caspian Sea, are the Alborz Mountains, and the western borders of modern Iraq, which run alongside the borders with Iraq and Turkey, are protected by the Zagros Mountains. Deserts dominate the topography in both central and southern Iran, with the plateau slowly rising toward the east to eventually form part of the great Himalayas. Figure 2 shows the topography of Iran and the surrounding region. Persis in ancient times would have been the region in southern Iran surrounding the modern-day city of Shiraz.

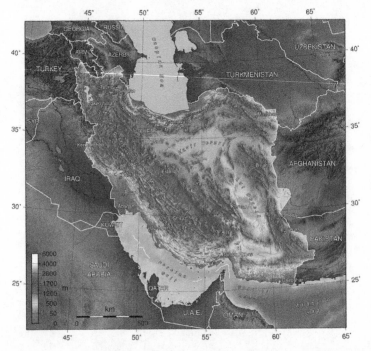

Because of this climate, locations for human settlement were scarce. Most fertile land existed in between mountaintops, and rainfall in the region was, and still is, minimal. The majority of the territory must rely on snow melts in the spring for their water supply, and securing this precious resource was, and still is, frequently at the top of the priority list for any leader in the region. Yet despite these difficulties, people were able to find ways to install and grow civilizations. But traditional agriculture was not common, with people making use of animal husbandry as their primary source of food and income.

However, because of their cultural and linguistic differences, and also because of the geopolitical situation at the time of their arrival in Iran, Persian history is very much defined by how they interacted with their more powerful and more influential neighbors.

With the founding of Pasargadae in the 7th century BCE, Assyria, which had been the dominant power in the region for much of the last 300 years, was on the brink of collapse. But it was still the most powerful empire in Mesopotamia and abroad; their sphere of influence extended as far west as Egypt and as far east as the Zagros Mountains. Assyrian records indicate that the first Persian kings, who held loose hegemony over the region of Persis, were vassals to the Assyrian kings, sending tribute to them as a sign of their fealty.

However, by the end of the 7th century BCE, Assyria would fall and all but disappear from the annals of history. But when this happened, new powers, specifically Babylon, Elam, Chaldaea, Lydia, Egypt, and to a lesser extent, Greece, were all flexing their muscles in western Asia, meaning right from the beginning the Persians would need to fight to maintain control over the territory they were to call home. That the Persian Empire would go down in history as one of the most militarily advanced should come as no surprise to students of history.

Yet this transition would not occur overnight. After the fall of Assyria, the Persians would become vassals to the Medes, who were gaining influence in the region and who helped the Babylonians, Elamites, and Egyptians topple the Assyrian Empire. But Persia was growing in both size and influence. It had begun to establish its own monarchic tradition, with one royal family, the Achaemenid, assuming complete control over the Persian throne. This family slowly grew in power, and in c. 550 BCE, Cyrus II, also known as Cyrus the Great, rose to power and succeeded in overthrowing Median rule, effectively giving Persia political autonomy, and birthing the first Persian Empire and dynasty, which would play an important role in shaping the region's history.

Conclusion

Overall, the Persians can be considered latecomers to the scene of Ancient Mesopotamia, Iran, and the Middle East. But this is not to discount their influence. Using the lens of historical hindsight, the

Persians arrived at a particularly fortuitous time in history. The fall of the Assyrians meant political turmoil in the region. And although the Neo-Babylonian Empire would take control over much of Mesopotamia, Iran and the surrounding region was up for the taking. The succession of kings in the Achaemenid Dynasty would bring great glory to the Persian people, and they would help cement the Persians as one of the most formidable, powerful, and influential civilizations in all of human history.

Chapter 2 – The Birth of the Achaemenid Empire: The Rise and Reign of Cyrus the Great

By the middle of the 6th century BCE, the political landscape in Mesopotamia and the surrounding area had changed considerably. Assyria was no more, and the alliance formed by two of its enemies—Babylon and Media—had thinned. Their relationship was tenuous, and after the spoils of the Assyrian Empire had been conquered, tensions began to rise once again.

At this time, different Persian tribes scattered throughout the region of Persis were beginning to unify and exert some form of national identity. This surge in nationalism came at the right time for the Persians, for political turmoil in the region meant the conditions for asserting their independence were rather favorable.

Establishing a Nation: The Unification of Persia

In 559 BCE, the first real momentous event in Persian history would take place: the crowning of Cyrus II, who would later be known as Cyrus II the Great. This moniker was likely given in recognition of his tremendous accomplishment: uniting the Persian tribes and expanding the Persian Empire to be the largest in the region at the time.

Cyrus II's capital was Pasargadae, and it was occupied largely by members of the Pasargadae tribe, which was ruled by Cyrus II's family, the Achaemenid. But at this moment in history, he would have been a vassal to the Median kings. Yet he was not satisfied with being relegated to the role of a secondary king, so he began to plot a revolt that would help the Persian people claim some degree of political autonomy.

He started by gathering the support of other Persian tribes that had settled throughout the Iranian plateau, namely the Maraphii, the Maspii, the Panthialaei, Deusiaei, and the Germanii. But Cyrus II knew he would be unable to overthrow Median rule completely on his own, so after succeeding in unifying many of the different Persian tribes, he began seeking out an ally to support him in his revolution.

As mentioned earlier, the warmness that defined Babylonian-Median affairs during their joint attempt to remove the Assyrians from their position of dominance had cooled considerably, and although the two powers were not in open conflict, they were also not good friends. As a result, Babylon would be Cyrus II's top choice as an ally, and considering Babylon was Persia's next closest neighbor not counting Media, this decision made logical sense.

At the time Cyrus II was plotting his revolt against his Median rulers, Babylonia was going through a transition. The Chaldaeans— an ethnic group that made up a large part of the Babylonian Empire—were always creating controversy regarding the Babylonian throne, for they were often not welcomed as leaders by other powers in the region; Assyria, Elam, and Media would frequently support revolts inside Babylon that came about as a result of a Chaldaean rising to the throne.

When Cyrus II was gathering support for his rebellion, Babylon did not have anyone with a clear claim to the throne. Eventually, an anti-

Chaldaean leader, Nabu-naid, was made king, and he made an alliance with Cyrus II to help him retake lands lost to the Medians during the wars with Assyria just the century before, specifically the region surrounding the city of Harran, which was the last city to fall in the Assyrian Empire, removing them from power in the region.

Cyrus II began his war against the Medians in 555 BCE, and the Babylonians did their part by expelling Medians from contested territories near the Persian Gulf. This occupied Median forces from both fronts, which made it far easier for Cyrus II and his armies to move into Median territory and conquer its cities, including its capital, Ecbatana. Efforts by the Medians to retaliate were thwarted by mutiny—their troops likely recognizing their imminent doom— and this meant that by 550 BCE Cyrus II had succeeded in conquering Media. Persia was now officially an independent nation, but its power and influence would in part derive from the close connections it had with the former Median Empire. Cyrus II essentially assumed control over what the Medians had already built, and he and his successors would expand upon that to firmly place the Persians at the center of this powerful Iranian civilization.

This is understandably a glorious moment in Persian history, but it would also set in motion a period of considerable uncertainty that the Persians would need to deal with to be able to maintain their newfound autonomy. Specifically, the conquest of the Median tribes meant that Cyrus II now felt he had the right to rule over territories once claimed by Median kings, which were spread out across Mesopotamia, Assyria, Syria, Armenia, and Cappadocia (a region in modern-day Turkey).

However, the Babylonians also felt they had legitimate claims to these lands, which put Persia immediately into conflict with a culture that had been its ally just several years before. As a result, these beginning stages of Persian history are closely tied to what the Babylonians were doing and how these two powerful kingdoms negotiated the absence of Media, which had previously served as a buffer between Babylon and other more powerful nations to the east.

But before Cyrus II would set to work on conquering the Babylonians and bringing southern Mesopotamia under his control, he would spend time in the north of the Fertile Crescent, which helped him extend Persian influence further westward.

Rising Power: The Conquest of Lydia

The remarkable thing about Cyrus II is that he went from being king of a powerful yet small city in the Iranian plateau to the emperor of a vast civilization stretching from his homeland to all the way west to Egypt in less than a lifetime. And his successors would go even further by reaching and engaging in battle with the outlying Greek city-states. Because of this, in just one generation, Persia went from being a collection of scattered tribes identifying with the same origins and speaking the same language to the largest empire ever seen in the Fertile Crescent and Mediterranean. In fact, it would become the largest empire in the world at the time, except for China.

When Cyrus came to power, he would have been called the King of Ashan, the name of the village from which he came, the one that would have given him his title and the right to rule. Little mention was made of the term "King of Persia" until much later in history, and it may have come from the name used by cultures from afar to describe a territory populated by different Persian tribes. The first mention of the King of Persia comes from Babylonian records, who would have recognized the change in power coming from one of their closest and most powerful allies.

After Cyrus II managed to conquer Media, he began to set his sights further afield, specifically toward the kingdoms of Lydia and Babylon. But it took him nearly three years to rally his troops and set out on campaign. There would have been resistance to Cyrus II's conquest, meaning some former Median subjects would have resisted giving fealty to Cyrus II, which would have required military operation. But once Cyrus II felt he had the situation sufficiently under control, he would have reorganized and set out on campaign.

The Lydian kingdom is located west of Media in central Turkey. (Figure 3 shows a map of how 6th century Iran and Mesopotamia may have been politically organized before the Persian rise to power).

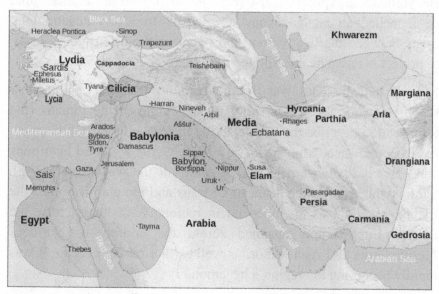

While not very powerful, the kingdom of Lydia was strategically located, particularly for its more powerful western neighbors, i.e., Greece and Egypt. Both saw Lydia as a useful buffer between themselves and the more powerful kingdoms that tended to come out of Mesopotamia. They likely would not have fully understood the extent of Persian power at this time, but after three centuries of Assyrian rulers, the leaders of Egyptian and Greek kingdoms knew to keep their distance. As a result, they were willing to offer support to the Lydians when they needed help defending themselves from eastern invaders.

Around 30 years before the rise of Cyrus II, Lydia and Media had signed a treaty to establish the boundary of Halys, which would divide Asia Minor (modern-day Turkey) among the Lydians and the Medians (see figure 3 above to find the border between these two kingdoms.) However, when Cyrus conquered the Medians in 550

BCE, the leaders of Lydia feared Cyrus II would not honor the terms of this treaty.

As a result, the Lydian king at the time, Croesus, sent to the Babylonians, Egyptians, and Greeks for help. And in the meantime, he launched an attack against Cyrus II, effectively negating the treaty between the two nations and going on the offensive as a way to protect his own people and territory.

Records indicate that Cyrus II's first response was to try and incite a rebellion inside Lydian territory by appealing to the Ionians (the term used to describe the Greeks living in Asia Minor), but this must have been unsuccessful, for in 547 BCE, Cyrus II rallied his troops and entered Lydian territory, advancing all the way to its capital, Sardis, which led to the death of Croesus and the elimination of the Lydian kingdom as an independent nation. With this victory, the Persian Empire now spanned across the entirety of Northern Mesopotamia and Asia Minor, as well as the Iranian plateau. It was rapidly becoming the region's hegemon.

What's interesting to note about the conquest of Lydia is that this would have brought together two very different cultures. When Cyrus II took control of Media, he was assuming power in a land full of people not exceptionally different from his own. They both spoke Iranian languages; they would have looked relatively similar, for both groups could trace their origins back to the Aryans of the north; and they practiced the same religion. However, when Cyrus conquered the Lydians, he brought people under his control who had been heavily influenced by Greek culture and Greek thinking. This would have made it a challenge for him to maintain control over the region. And it also helps show why Cyrus II would have been inclined to treat Greek customs or beliefs as something less than his own. The Persians and Greeks have a long history together defined by conflict and rivalry, and it's possible this came from the initial cultural shock Cyrus II would have experienced upon riding into Asia Minor and claiming the lands of Lydia as part of the Persian Empire.

Solidifying Control: The Conquest of Babylon

After managing to secure control of the Lydians, Cyrus II had managed to grow the size of the Persian Empire considerably. Its sphere of influence in 547 BCE would have included the Iranian plateau and its surrounding territories, including the lands previously controlled by the Medians, as well as the Lydian kingdom. At this point in the story, though, Neo-Babylonia and Egypt remain independent, but they would soon have to face advances from Cyrus II's powerful army.

Egypt would likely have felt more secure since an invasion into their territory would have required Cyrus II and his army to cross through Syria and Phoenicia, territories still loyal to the Babylonian throne. Yet the Babylonian king would have recognized his peril.

However, he would have to wait nearly seven years for the fighting to begin. It's unclear what Cyrus II was doing during these years. It would have made sense to simply continue his advance southward from Lydia into Babylon, but something took his attention away. There is some speculation that he had to attend to matters in the furthest eastern parts of the newly formed empire, but these facts have not been confirmed.

Nevertheless, when Cyrus II did finally organize an attack into Babylon in 540 BCE, it seemed the time spent in between the two campaigns had given him the chance to properly prepare for the invasion. Cyrus II would march into Babylon and be able to call himself king within the year, meaning that by 539 BCE, the Neo-Babylonian Empire had fallen.

Part of the reason Cyrus II was able to be so successful in his invasion is because of internal strife that existed among the different rulers within Babylon. A long-time source of conflict within Babylonian affairs were the Chaldaeans. This ethnic group claimed to be the "true Babylonians," and they used these assertions to grant themselves power over the land. However, other groups did not see things this way, and there were constant struggles between Chaldaeans and other ethnic groups throughout Babylonian history. Cyrus II incited anti-Chaldaean sentiment upon his invasion and was able to win the support of many Babylonian citizens, making his invasion much easier.

But Cyrus II must have recognized that although he was now the king of Babylon, maintaining that title would require close control over this once very powerful group of people. As a result, he installed himself in the palace of Babylonian royalty, added the title King of Babylon to his, and also appointed his son, Cambyses, governor of Babylon, so as to give him tighter control over the region.

Conclusion: The Death of Cyrus II

After his successful conquest of Babylon, the next logical target would have been Egypt to the west. Control of Babylon gave Cyrus II a claim to both Syrian and Phoenician lands, and it seemed as though he would face little resistance in solidifying control in these regions. But this westward expansion would not occur while Cyrus II would be alive. His last ten years as king were spent building up his new empire and consolidating power, and when he died in 529 BCE, his son Cambyses took over as the new king of Persia, and he would be the one to enter Egypt.

As a conqueror, it's important to put Cyrus II's achievements in perspective. In the course of just 30 years, Cyrus II took loosely connected Persian tribes and unified them in an effort to assert autonomy over their Median rulers. But once he did this, he immediately embarked on a campaign of expansion that rivals any other in history. By the time of his death, the Median, Lydian, and Babylonian Empires, some of the most powerful in the ancient world, had been wiped off the face of the earth for good, and they were now closely controlled by Cyrus and his newfound Persian Empire. This remarkable expansion makes it easy to understand why

Persian historians look back and call their first true leader Cyrus the Great.

Chapter 3 – The Glory of the Achaemenid Empire: Cambyses & Darius

Cyrus II, or Cyrus the Great, unified Persia and then set out on military conquests that would make it western Asia's largest empire at the time. However, as any student of ancient history knows, successful conquest does not mean a successful empire. Once lands and kingdoms have been subjugated, there is a period of consolidation in which kings establish themselves as the true ruler of a territory.

However, this oftentimes is not the job of the king who does the conquering. Instead, it's typically his successors who manage to fortify the gains made by the conqueror, and their success in doing this determines whether these conquests result in the formation of an empire capable of lasting more than a generation or if they will disappear into the annals of history as a mere detour in some other civilization's path to power.

The two kings who came after Cyrus II, his son, Cambyses II, and Darius I, a potential pretender who managed to win the Persian crown despite facing frequent insurrections, were able to follow up on the first Persian emperor's successes. Cambyses II managed to expand the empire even further, and then Darius I, who ruled for much longer, fortified these gains and set up an imperial administration that would put Persia in a position for sustained hegemony. The Achaemenid Dynasty started as nothing more than a few kings who ruled over one Persian tribe, but by the end of Darius I's rule, it would be one of the most powerful dynasties in the history of both Persia and the entire ancient world.

The Reign of Cambyses II

When Cyrus II's son Cambyses took the throne in 529 BCE, the obvious next step for the Persian Empire was to continue west. Egypt had long been a prized possession for the civilizations of Mesopotamia and Iran. The kings of both Assyria and Babylonia sought to bring Egyptian territory under their control, and while both managed to do this, neither could maintain power for very long.

So, with Cambyses now at the head of western Asia's most powerful empire, it only makes sense that he would have turned to Egypt as his next target of conquest. However, like his father, he did not start this campaign until three years after he assumed control of the empire. It's unclear what he was doing, but it's believed tensions on the eastern borders of the Persian Empire kept his attention elsewhere.

Using Palestine and Syria as a path into Egypt, Cambyses and his army took the Gaza road west into Egypt to begin their invasion in 525 BCE. Their first target was the city of Pelusium, which was housing an Egyptian army. A decisive victory sent Egyptian forces running to nearby Memphis, which was the Egyptian capital at the time. The Persians would lay siege to the city, which eventually ended in its demise. The Egyptian king, Psammetichus III, was captured, and Cambyses was officially recognized as the king of Egypt.

On the heel of this victory, Cambyses continued his campaigning into Egypt and other parts of Africa. The kingdoms of Libya and Cyrene submitted to Cambyses, pushing his circle of influence further west. And employing Thebes as a base, he dispatched a massive force to follow the Nile River south into Ethiopia. Most historians think he was looking to extend Persian control as far west as Carthage (modern-day Tunisia), as well as into Ethiopia and to the Oasis of Ammon, known today as the Siwa (Siwah) Oasis (see figure 4).

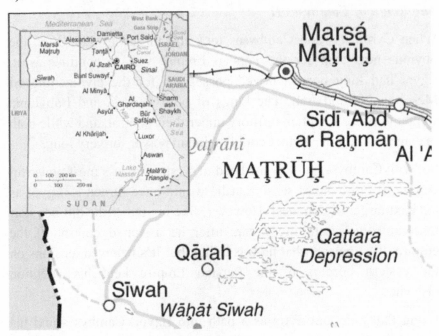

While the submission of Libya and Cyrene got Cambyses closer to Carthage and Siwa, he did not make it there. The force he sent was stopped, with most records indicating they succumbed to disaster, which was most likely a sandstorm. Cambyses himself would stall in his invasion of Ethiopia. Despite a large force of 50,000 men, Cambyses never managed to reach the Ethiopian capital of Meroe, which would have been necessary if Cambyses had wanted to claim control over the territory. It's unclear exactly why Cambyses could not make it all the way, but the belief is that a combination of the hot, humid Nile river climate and the lack of adequate supplies would have put considerable strain on Cambyses and his soldiers. Nevertheless, Cambyses had made significant additions to the Persian Empire, with its influence now extending throughout Egypt and toward its next most powerful neighbors, Carthage and Ethiopia, although these powers continued to enjoy their independence.

The Rise of Darius

Cambyses died in 522 BCE, just seven years after he assumed the throne. But in this short time, he had managed to expand the Persian Empire to its largest point, meaning his successor would be taking over a growing empire.

However, his death created significant turmoil within the empire that would have a lasting effect on its history. To understand this turmoil, one must place Cambyses' death in a larger context. Specifically, one must understand the rights to govern in Ancient Persia as well as the family tree of the ruling family, as this plays a big part in the stability of the empire.

To begin, remember that Cambyses and Cyrus II are part of the Achaemenid Dynasty, which gets its name from the Achaemenid clan, the most powerful clan and leader of the Pasargadae tribe, which is credited with the founding of the city of Pasargadae and also the unification of the different Persian tribes scattered throughout the Iranian plateau. The name Achaemenid likely comes from Achaemenes, who would have been Cyrus II's great-great-great-great grandfather. Figure 5 shows the Achaemenid family tree.

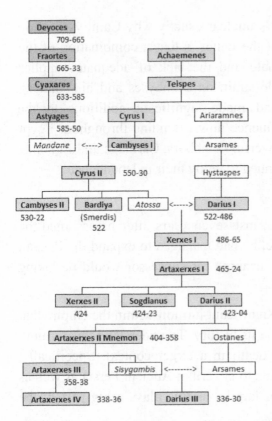

```
Deyoces
  709-665
Fraortes                    Achaemenes
  665-33
Cyaxares                    Teispes
  633-585
Astyages      Cyrus I       Ariaramnes
  585-50
Mandane <----> Cambyses I   Arsames
    Cyrus II    550-30       Hystaspes
Cambyses II  Bardiya  Atossa <-----> Darius I
  530-22    (Smerdis)              522-486
              522
                      Xerxes I    486-65
                      Artaxerxes I  465-24
Xerxes II   Sogdianus   Darius II
  424       424-23       423-04
    Artaxerxes II Mnemon  404-358   Ostanes
Artaxerxes III   Sisygambis <--------> Arsames
  358-38
Artaxerxes IV   338-36     Darius III   336-30
```

As a result, the legitimacy of any Persian's claim to the throne depended on his ability to trace his lineage back through the Achaemenid family tree all the way to Achaemenes himself. The figure above shows that Cyrus II had three children, Cambyses II, who would succeed Cyrus II and expand upon his imperial achievements, Bardiya, and Atossa, who was a woman and therefore disqualified from being able to take over for her father.

Bardiya died in 522 BCE, the same year Cambyses died and Darius I took over as king. But the circumstances surrounding his death are unclear. Some legends say Cambyses II lost his mind and killed his brother, and then died from a battle wound. Whereas other accounts differ, suggesting he died of natural causes. However, no matter what happened, the main point is that Cambyses II died without any clear heir, which naturally sprung the empire into turmoil as different people attempted to assert their right to rule.

Two different men would lay claim to the throne: Darius I and a man named Guatama, who is presumed to be a member of the Persian nobility but who had no real connection to the Achaemenid line. Both men would accuse the other of being a pretender. Guatama claimed he was in fact Bardiya and therefore the true heir of Cyrus II and the Persian throne. However, Darius I claimed Guatama was pretending to be Bardiya, since Bardiya was dead, and that he was using Persian ignorance of this death as a way of legitimizing his claim to the throne. Since Darius I was the oldest living kin of Achaemenes, he believed this was enough to justify his claim to the throne.

But while Darius I was adamant the man claiming to be Bardiya was an impostor, he was initially unable to convince many of the different regions under Persian control that this was the case. Several different kingdoms, such as Babylon, Lydia, and Media, all pledged fealty to Guatama/Bardiya at first. Yet in 522 BCE, Darius, along with the help of several Persian nobles, raided Guatama's capital and killed him, wiping away his claim to the throne and giving Darius I the opportunity to assert himself as the Persian sovereign. But because so many different kingdoms within the Persian Empire had declared fealty to Guatama/Bardiya, this event triggered a series of revolts that would come to define the early stages of Darius I's rule.

However, while brief, the reign of Guatama was quite peculiar, largely because even though Darius considered Guatama to be a pretender, he simultaneously recognized him as king of the land. Writing after the death of Guatama, Darius mentions how he took "his kingdom," making no reference to restoring himself to a kingdom he thought rightfully his. Some scholars have speculated that this is proof that Darius I was the pretender and that Guatama was indeed Bardiya and therefore a legitimate king, but no one has ever been able to confirm this theory with any degree of certainty.

It's likely, though, that Darius I took this approach as a response to Guatama's popularity. As an attempt to ingratiate himself with the people of the Persian Empire, a move he hoped would help convince them to pledge allegiance to him and to accept his rule, Guatama granted considerable freedoms to the Persian nobility and populace.

For example, he granted all the people in conquered territories freedom from military service and tribute for three years, something that would been welcomed by all. He also set out building temples according to the various religions in the region, and he worked with nobles and other powerful families from around the empire who had fallen in stature since conquest but who were interested in regaining their position of prominence. All of these moves meant that Guatama, although a "false" ruler in that he had not direct relation to Cyrus, became quite popular.

As a result, when Darius I managed to kill Guatama and place himself atop the Persian throne, he found himself in a position where he desperately needed to consolidate his own power, a process that would dominate much of the early part of his rule. Many leaders, such as those in Babylon, saw this as their moment to break free from Persian rule and to obtain their own independence. So, starting in 522 BCE and continuing for the next three years, Darius I would be primarily occupied with defeating the various rebellions that were breaking out across the empire and confirming his position as the one and only Persian king. Later on, once he had managed to bring the different parts of his empire back under his control, he would marry Atossa, the daughter of Cyrus, and the children they bore together would continue the Achaemenid line.

Darius the Conqueror

Unlike his two predecessors, Darius I was not as concerned with expanding the empire. The circumstances of his ascension meant he needed to spend considerable time campaigning throughout the interior of the empire so as to consolidate the monarchy. But once he managed to secure his grip on power, he began looking to stretch the limits of Persian influence in the region. However, his gains were significantly more modest than either of the two kings who came before him as well as the more prominent ones who came after him.

Upon taking the throne, Darius I immediately had to deal with rebellion. His contention claim meant not all provinces of the empire supported him. As a result, his first order of business was tending to unrest in Susiana, the name given to the territory that had previously been the kingdom of Elam, which was in open rebellion.

(Figure 6 shows where Susiana was in relation to Persia and its capital at Pasargadae.)

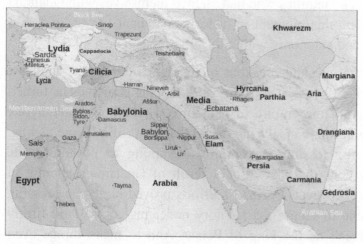

However, this revolt would not last long, and Darius was able to quell it by sending an army to the city. He entrusted this campaign to his generals and did not accompany them, suggesting he did not consider the chances of defeat to be very high.

The next revolt he had to deal with, though, did a much better job at capturing the attention of Darius I. Babylon, which had declared fealty to Guatama, had hoped to use this climate of political instability to their favor and win their independence back from the Persians. And since Babylon was a powerful city in the region that any emperor looking to expand needed to control, Darius I would have considered this rebellion far more important.

Darius I gathered and led an army into Babylon to quell the rebellion and establish himself as the true ruler of the land. And while the Babylonians put up a stronger resistance compared to the Susians, their revolt did not last long, and by 521 BCE they had surrendered their claims to independence and declared loyalty to Darius I, which once again made Babylon a province of the Persian Empire.

For the next year or so, Darius I would be consumed by his attempts to consolidate his power and bring the kingdoms conquered by Cyrus and Cambyses more firmly under his control. Besides Susiana and Babylon, Darius faced rebellions in Media, Armenia, and within Persia itself. The families who had aligned themselves with Guatama were also using this moment in history as a chance to try and gain more power and autonomy within the empire.

Because of the constant breakout of rebellions during the first few years of Darius I's rule, it was almost as though as soon as he turned to one corner of the empire to put down a rebellion, another one broke out somewhere else. This meant that most of his time as king was spent crisscrossing the empire attempting to put down the various rebellions that started as a result of Guatama's attempt to claim power. However, Darius I's efforts proved largely successful, as he was able to secure the territory under his control and firmly establish himself as the king of Persia. And to make things even more clear, he married Atossa, the daughter of Cyrus II, meaning their children would be able to claim they were direct descendants of this famous king and therefore legitimate rulers of Persia.

The other major concern of Darius I's rule was Egypt. After having recently been conquered by Cambyses, it was up to Darius I to hold power over Egypt in any way possible. And because Egypt was considered to be a conquered territory, the main tactic for maintaining political control was force. Darius I himself did not spend much time in Egypt—he was far too busy working to maintain control of other imperial lands—but he did dedicate quite a bit of military energy to the region. He appointed a general and an admiral to control the army and naval fleet that was stationed in Memphis, giving them the task of upholding Persian rule while Darius was occupied elsewhere.

However, despite force being the primary tactic for consolidating power in Egypt, Darius undertook a number of other policies that demonstrated his understanding of just how difficult it would be to keep this great power subjugated to Persian rule. For example, he practiced a rather high level of religious tolerance, giving the Egyptians free reign to practice their religion, which would have come as a welcome respite from the rather intolerant policies of Cambyses.

Darius I also invested considerably in the economic welfare of Egypt, primarily by building canals and dams, the most prominent being a canal which connected the Nile to the Red Sea, something that would have opened up trade considerably for the Egyptians. Darius also limited the tribute demands he made on Egyptian kings, which would have reduced the burden of living under Persian rule and kept people from attempting rebellion. These policies in Egypt helped Darius I keep Egypt relatively subdued while his attention was drawn elsewhere in the empire.

But because Darius had to spend so much of his time dealing with rebellions within the empire, he spent little time expanding its borders. This is a common theme when studying major empires throughout history: the empire is expanded by one or two kings, and the next few successors are left with the task of consolidating those gains and strengthening control over newly conquered territories.

However, Darius I did manage to slightly expand the borders of the Persian Empire, although it's best to think of these conquests more as reconquests of territory that either Cyrus or Cambyses had managed to take over but that had wriggled free of Persian control when Cambyses died.

As Figure 7 shows, he was able to push Persian influence closer to Carthage, although he did not quite get all the way there. And he was also able to expand west through Turkey, leaving the Persians at the northern borders of Greek territory. This move would define Persian history in many ways. The next king, Xerxes, spent most of his time attempting to conquer Greece, and the Greco-Persian Wars were a major influence in Persian and world history.

But perhaps Darius' significant achievements as a conqueror took place on the eastern frontiers of the empire. His armies reached as far east as the Indus River, and Darius was able to extract tribute from the kings ruling in those territories, bringing the Persians as far east as they would ever manage to go.

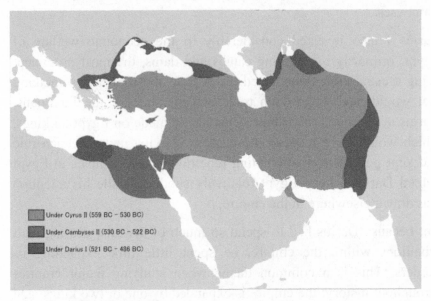

Under Cyrus II (559 BC – 530 BC)
Under Cambyses II (530 BC – 522 BC)
Under Darius I (521 BC – 486 BC)

The Greco-Persian Wars

As the two most powerful kingdoms in western Asia and the Fertile Crescent, Greek and Persian history, especially during the Achaemenid Dynasty, are closely intertwined. Greece was always a target for the Persian conquerors of the Achaemenid Dynasty, largely because it, along with Egypt, was the most culturally advanced in the region. The successes of Cyrus II and Cambyses II in invading both gave Darius I, hope for being able to finally conquer the Greek city-states and bring them under the control of the Persian Empire.

However, the Greeks had other plans, and the series of battles and revolts that took place during the first half of the 5th century BCE are known as the Greco-Persian Wars. Various cities and kingdoms aligned themselves with each side, turning this conflict into a bloody, long-lasting war that would dramatically reshape the power structures in the region and subsequently the history of both civilizations.

To understand this war, which is best understood as a series of heightened military conflicts between Greece and Persia (we could look at it as a series of wars, but in historical context they all belong to one conflict), it's important to remember the nature of Greece at this time. While the Greeks would soon form one of the largest empires in the history of the world, at this point in time there was no unified Greece. Instead, Greece was best understood as a combination of city-states that shared a language. Commerce was a defining characteristic of early Greek civilization, with these large, influential city-states engaging in considerable trade amongst themselves. Because of this, several of these city-states became rather wealthy and powerful on their own, making it difficult for the Persians to effectively exert control over them.

The year 499 BCE is generally regarded as the beginning of the Greco-Persian Wars. This was the year when Aristagoras, the tyrant king of the Greek city-state Miletus, which is on the western coast of Anatolia, combined forces with Darius I to invade and conquer the island of Naxos. However, this failed, and Aristagoras knew that Darius I would likely punish him and maybe even remove him from power as a result of his failed military campaign. So, in an attempt to retain his own power, Aristagoras turned on Darius I and encouraged all the peoples of Hellenic (Greek) Asia Minor to revolt against the Persians. He was largely successful, and this started a period known as the Ionian Revolts, which lasted until 493 BCE.

But these revolts would not end without first causing serious harm to Persian power in the region. Aristagoras was able to secure military support for his actions from both Athens and Eretria, and together they managed to sack and burn the Persian capital in Asia Minor, Sardis.

This move obviously sparked a good deal of anger from Darius I, and he set out to avenge his lost territory. Because Athens and Eritrea had joined with Aristagoras in the attack, this set the Persian king's sights firmly on mainland Greece. The first target in Darius I's campaign was Miletus itself, the center of Aristagoras' power, and after several years of stalemate, Darius I was able to beat the Ionians (the term used for the Greeks settled along the western coast of Asia Minor) at the decisive Battle of Lade.

Determined to fully punish those who had been responsible for the political upheaval in Ionia and Asia Minor, Darius I began to plan a full-scale invasion of Greece with the goal of conquering those who lent support to Aristagoras, Athens and Eretria. Darius I gave leadership of the Greek campaign to General Mardonius, who succeeded in bringing the cities of Thrace and Macedon back under Persian control. He was then beaten back in his attempts to advance, bringing his progress to a halt in 490 BCE.

The Persians set to the seas and sailed across the Aegean, and during this campaign they were able to conquer Cyclades, and they were even able to capture Eretria, burning it to the ground. Having succeeded in entering deep into Greek territory in less than 10 years after the beginning of the Ionian Revolts, the Persians continued their march toward Athens. Yet, they were met by the Athenians and fought the Battle of Marathon, which the Greeks won, effectively stopping the Persians in their tracks. Figure 8 shows a map of the various movements of the Persian and Greek armies during the Ionian Revolts and subsequent Greco-Persian Wars.

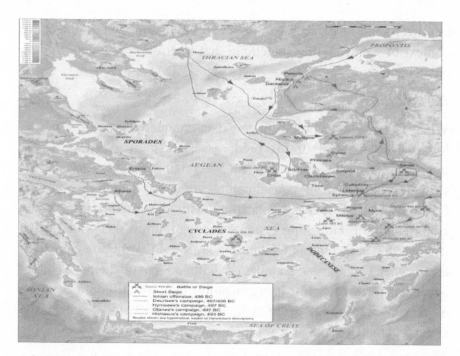

After his defeat at the Battle of Marathon, Darius I began to regather his forces for a second attempt at an invasion, but he died in 486 BCE, leaving the responsibility of Greek conquest to his son, Xerxes. But these events would end up having a significant impact on the future of both the Greeks and the Persians. For one, it helped solidify anti-Persian sentiment among the Greeks. For example, Sparta, which had remained relatively neutral during the conflicts, now came out and declared a desire to free the Greek people from Persian bother. They would join forces with Athens and other Greek city-states to form the Delian League, which would play a crucial role in attempting to undermine Persian power throughout its entire empire by inciting rebellion and waging war.

The Delian League would be active for the next 30 or so years, and their part of the story ends when the League failed to incite an effective coup in Egypt. By 450 BCE, the Greco-Persian Wars slowly cooled and eventually ended, but not before both cultures had dramatically influenced each other's history. The reign of Xerxes would be almost entirely defined by his campaigns against Greece, but this period of Persian history is best understood within the entire context of Xerxes' rule, something that is discussed in detail in the next chapter.

Darius I the King

While Darius I's accomplishments as a conqueror are not nearly as impressive as those of his predecessors, this was not the most important thing to come out of his reign. Possibly due to the struggles he faced in consolidating and establishing his power, Darius I was particularly concerned with the organization of the empire and in establishing systems and institutions that would make it easier for both him and future kings to hold dominion over their territory. What Darius I came up with ended up being a rather advanced form of political organization that would continue to be used even after the fall of the Achaemenid Dynasty to Alexander the Great and the Greeks in the 4th century BCE.

The first decision Darius I made as king in terms of the empire's organization was which type of government to use. Darius I gathered his closest advisers to discuss what would be the best way for establishing and maintaining control over what had now become a vast, expansive empire. Darius I was in favor of a monarchy, whereas some of his advisers advocated for a republic, and some even came out in support of an oligarchy. In the end, Darius I was able to convince his counsel, and the Persian government officially became an absolute monarchy with Darius I as its sovereign. This monarchy would be hereditary, something that would have been important to Persians at the time, as evidenced by both Darius I and Guatama's attempt to establish their Achaemenid lineage.

The next decision he needed to make was where to place his capital. Pasargadae had been the capital of Cyrus II, but shortly after ascending to the throne, Darius I began constructing palaces and temples in Persepolis in 521 BCE, which was not too far to the north of Pasargadae. Part of the reason both of these kings chose to build their capitals in this region is that this was considered the Persian core territory. Choosing these locations as the center of the empire would have been a source of great pride for the Persians living in that territory, and since the Persian kings depended on the Persians themselves to form their vast armies and conduct their extensive military campaigns, pleasing these people would have been a top priority for both Cyrus II and Darius I.

But while it made symbolic and cultural sense to build the Persian capital deep in the heart of Persis, it did not make much sense in terms of the administration of the empire. Both cities were hidden away among the mountainous terrain of the Iranian plateau, which would have made them difficult to connect to the rest of the empire. As a result, Darius I began constructing another capital at the same time Persepolis was being build.

This city, Susa, located in northwestern Iran, was much closer to the large political and cultural centers of the Persian Empire, Babylon and Ecbatana (the former capital of the Median Empire and an important city for the administration of the empire and the lands formerly controlled by the Medes). It would have been much easier to connect Susa to the network of roads that had been built throughout western Asia, making it much easier for the monarch to communicate with his generals and governors who would have been spread throughout Persian-controlled territory. However, Persepolis would remain the cultural center of the empire, and while Darius I chose to be buried there, he would have spent almost no time in the city.

The other major thing Darius I did was organize the empire into satrapies, which were essentially provinces. Most records indicate Darius created 20 different satrapies throughout the empire, the most prominent being centered in Egypt (Memphis), Babylon, Arabia, Asia Minor (modern-day Turkey), Ecbatana and Media, and Bactria, which is the territory to the northeast of Persia in modern-day Afghanistan. Figure 9 shows a map of what the Persian Empire would have looked like under Darius I. At this time, the Achaemenid Dynasty-controlled Persia was at its largest point in history.

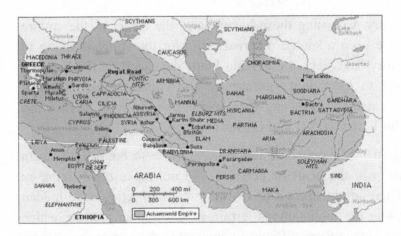

While the division of his administration into provinces was nothing new, Darius I did two things that set him apart and helped him secure a stronger grip on power. First, he gave satraps (the leaders of the satrapies) rather significant freedom in the management of their provinces. While the king's word was law in all the land, the satraps were capable of speaking on behalf of the king, serving as the high judge in the region. Furthermore, the satraps were independently responsible for securing their territory. Revolts or rebellions were dealt with directly by the satraps, and this may have allowed for more effective responses; previous empires in the regions, namely Assyria, launched military campaigns and deported large numbers of people whenever there was a rebellion. But the Persians favored a more localized response, which would have helped quiet hostilities toward the king in Persia.

The second thing Darius I did in setting up his satrapies and government was to enact a policy of religious tolerance. The Persian Empire at the time of Darius I stretched as far west as Asia Minor and even parts of mainland Greece, down to Egypt, Libya, and Sudan, across Arabia and Mesopotamia, and all the way east to the Indus River. As a result, there was a great deal of diversity in terms of cultural and religious traditions. And instead of attempting to crush these and replace them with Persian customs, Darius I left people's cultures intact and even contributed to their growth by assisting in the building of temples and other buildings that would have facilitated worship.

These two features of the Persian government—decentralization and tolerance—were not nearly as prominent in other western Asian governments, and it's likely this helped contribute to the rise of Persian dominance. Previous empires in the region, such as Assyria or Babylon, struggled to maintain political stability largely because of the vast regional diversity. However, Darius I was able to set up a system that left regional customs intact but that also allowed for Darius I to easily and effectively assert his power over the various dominions of the empire.

Conclusion

The significance of the rules of Cambyses II and Darius I cannot be overlooked. While Cambyses II only ruled for seven years, he was successful in following his father, Cyrus the Great, in expanding the reaches of the empire further west into Africa and parts of southeastern Europe. Darius I's much longer, yet somewhat less eventful, rule helped to consolidate these gains and set up a system of government that would allow the Persian Empire to flourish as western Asia's greatest power. At the time of Darius I's death and the ascension of his son Xerxes, the empire was at its largest point and poised for further growth.

Yet the Achaemenid Dynasty's power was rapidly reaching its apex, and before too long it would begin to fall apart until it eventually fell in the 4th century BCE to the Greeks. However, this would not happen until after the Persians managed to cement themselves as a regional power that would stand the test of time, and also contribute significantly to the cultural development of not only the region but the entire ancient world.

Chapter 4 – The Beginning of the End: The Reign of Xerxes and the Downfall of the Achaemenid Dynasty

Perhaps the most famous of all of the Persian kings, Xerxes the Great rose to the throne after his father. Two generations of rule, starting with Cyrus II and continuing through to Darius I, had expanded the Persian Empire to its largest point. It was undoubtedly the most powerful civilization in western Asia, and the Greco-Persian Wars indicated that Europe was not safe either. However, Xerxes would depart from some of the policies enacted by his father. This would help to amplify his power and importance, but it also increased the chances of regional revolt and dissension, a common "thorn in the side" of nearly all ancient rulers.

As a result of this policy change that was designed to help consolidate power, the power of the Persians, or more specifically the Achaemenids, was beginning to slip ever so slightly, even though Xerxes inherited an empire at its peak. He would not lose considerable territory, but he would not make large gains either. And his famed failure in invading Greece and Europe would dramatically alter the course of Persian history. But despite his eccentricities and only modest successes, Xerxes was still the most powerful man in all of western Asia, and he would go down as one of the most formidable kings in the history of humanity.

Xerxes Ascends to the Throne and Secures His Empire

It was Persian tradition that the king name a successor before embarking on a long military campaign, and so the decision to name Xerxes crown prince came when Darius I's son was still just a boy. The decision to name Xerxes as his heir was somewhat surprising considering Xerxes was not Darius I's oldest son, since Persian tradition called for appointing the eldest son as the heir to a father's wealth and titles. This was because Darius I's oldest son was not born into royalty. Instead, he came about from a relationship Darius I had with a commoner before he himself became king. But shortly after winning the throne from Guatama the Pretender, Darius I married Cyrus II's daughter, Atossa, and their first child, Xerxes, was considered to be Darius I's eldest royal son, making him the ideal choice to take over the kingdom.

As crown prince, Xerxes would lead the satrapy of Babylon. He was given the title king of Babylon, and this was used as his training for when he would eventually become king of the entire empire.

Some of the behavior of Xerxes, such as repurposing religious buildings in Persepolis to become harems, suggest that the Persian kingdom was beginning to mature. Three straight kings had been able to conquer and hold large swaths of territory, and this allowed the royalty to become quite rich. They spent these riches on their cities and palaces, attempting to build them up to be fitting of the splendor of the larger empire.

But just because the Persian Empire had grown significantly in power and size since the time of Cyrus II, it did not mean that Xerxes inherited a unified country at peace with itself. His father's campaigns into Greece had been stalled after his defeat at the Battle of Marathon, and while he was regrouping for a second invasion, revolt broke out in Egypt. And to the east, the Bactrians, named for the province of Bactra, a region located to the east of Persia in the modern-day nations of Afghanistan, Uzbekistan, and Tajikistan, were also creating unrest and threatening to try and break free from Persian rule.

Because of their close proximity, revolt in Egypt was also usually followed by revolt in Jerusalem. And this was also the case in 485 BCE when Xerxes was ascending to the Persian throne. As a result, his first act as king would be to move against Palestine and Egypt to quell their rebellion and bring both regions back under firm control. By 484 BCE, Xerxes and his armies marched across Palestine and through Gaza to Egypt, and they were able to quickly and effectively put down the revolt that had broken out.

However, despite how quickly this campaign began and ended, Xerxes' actions in Egypt would have a lasting effect on the empire and its ability to control the regions its kings had conquered. This starts with Xerxes' response to this Egyptian revolt, as it shows a departure from the ruling style of his father, Darius I.

Darius I showed great respect for Egyptian religion and customs, and he went out of his way to make sure they had the chance to practice their culture. He recognized and even honored some of the Egyptian gods, and he even went so far as to take an Egyptian god-king name for himself so as to keep in line with Egyptian understanding of monarchical rule. However, Xerxes was not nearly as tolerant, choosing instead to reject the religious practices of the Egyptians and to try and get them to adjust to Persian customs. These efforts were largely unsuccessful and would make it difficult for Xerxes to maintain tight control over the Egyptians.

The other major issues Xerxes had to deal with upon gaining power was Babylon. Since he had served as viceroy in this ancient capital while his father was king, Xerxes initially had no trouble in securing support for his claim to be the sovereign in Babylon. However, a curious decision to change the titles associated with the Persian king helped stir some doubt about the legitimacy of Xerxes' claim to power.

Because of its historical significance in the region, the Persian kings before Xerxes would refer to themselves, especially and perhaps only when addressing the Babylonian people, as "King of Babylon, king of lands." This was in part to try and pay respect to this ancient power, but it was also a strategic move; all empires in Mesopotamia and western Asia needed a plan for how they would appease the kings and citizens of Babylon. And since Babylon was at its lowest point in terms of regional power when Persia rose to prominence, these small formalities were enough to keep the Babylonians content.

However, when Xerxes became king, he would quickly do an about-face, and this would have a major effect on the beginning of his rule. As viceroy, he had managed to gain considerable support, and there was no contest to his claim to the throne at first. But when addressing the Babylonians in the early days of his kingship, he referred to himself as Xerxes, "King of Parsa (Persia) and Mada (Media)," choosing to relegate "King of Babylon, king of lands" to the end of his title, something that would have been greatly insulting to the Babylonian people, especially their rulers.

Some scholars speculate that this move was not folly, but rather an intentional move to try and strip Babylon of some of its independence. After what had just happened in Egypt, Xerxes was likely beginning to doubt the effectiveness of his father's hands-off policies, and this humiliation of the Babylonians may have had the intended effect of reasserting himself as the one and only sovereign in Babylon.

No matter the intention, the effect of Xerxes' decision was initially chaos. Seeing a break in the people's fealty to Xerxes, a powerful member of the Babylonian nobility, Belshimanni, rose up and attempted to claim independence for Babylon and its people. He addressed himself as "King of Babylon, king of lands," a clear attempt to ingratiate himself with the Babylonian people in a way Xerxes had refused to do. Belshimanni started by storming the Persian installations in Babylon, and he managed to reach and kill the satrap that had been appointed by Xerxes to manage Babylon and its surrounding territories.

Fortunately for Xerxes, and unfortunately for Belshimanni, the Persian king, who was in Ecbatana at the time, had access to his best general, his brother-in-law, Megabyzus. Under command of Xerxes, he took an army to Babylon and quickly destroyed Belshimanni and his rebellion. He moved swiftly and decisively, taking Babylon back in just a matter of days. And then he set about to punish the Babylonians for their insurrection. He destroyed the city wall, tore down temples and other religious buildings, and he also melted down the 18-foot gold statue of Bel Marduk, one of the Babylonian's most important gods, into bullion, killing all the priests and other people who attempted to protest it.

This prompt change in policy regarding how the different satraps would be managed began to reshape the direction of Persian history. As one might expect, it began to sow the seeds for rebellion throughout the empire, which any student of ancient history knows is the beginning of the end. And with Xerxes about to mount a massive invasion of Greece and Europe, the destiny of the Achaemenid Dynasty is slowly beginning to come into question. But for those living contemporaneously, it would not have seemed this way. The Persian army was still as strong as ever, and Xerxes' harsh response to insurrection would have struck fear in people across the empire, discouraging dissent and strengthening Xerxes' control over western Asia.

Xerxes Moves on Greece

What's interesting about Xerxes, and something that separates him quite a bit from his father Darius I and his uncle Cambyses, is that he was not particularly interested in conquest. Xerxes would have been the first Persian king to be born into the tremendous splendor that came from the imperial gains made by his forefathers, so it's only natural he concerned himself with other interests, namely the fortification of his power and the glorification of his wealth within the empire.

For example, once Xerxes took over as king, he immediately began overseeing the massive construction projects started by his father. He put finishing touches on the palaces that had been started by Darius I in Babylon and Susa, and he also went to work completing the splendid terraces surrounding his father's principal palace in Persepolis.

But despite his aversion to conquest and war, Xerxes would be unable to avoid a military campaign. And the obvious location for Xerxes' primary campaign was Greece and Europe. Darius I had intensified the Greco-Persian Wars by retaliating to the Ionian Revolts with a full-scale invasion of Greece. He managed to make it onto the Greek mainland and was headed for Athens when he was stopped and driven back across the Aegean Sea to Anatolia and Asia Minor.

However, it would take some convincing to get Xerxes to commit to a full-scale invasion of Greece, and also a little trickery. Persian diplomats who had been living in Athens had been exiled after Darius I's failed invasion. Desiring revenge, they hired an already discredited oracle to come and speak to Xerxes about the need to invade the Greeks again, and Xerxes' cousin, Mardonius, who was eager to get himself named satrap, egged Xerxes on, for newly conquered territory would have meant a need for new satraps.

As a result, Xerxes' destiny was altered and he began to turn his attention away from his personal enrichment and toward the expansion of the empire. Knowing how difficult it would be to successfully invade Greece and learning from his father's mistakes, Xerxes began planning a gradual advance that would take time and resources but that would also greatly increase his chances of success. For the invasion, he summoned the naval fleets of Egypt, Phoenicia, and the conquered Greeks in Asia Minor. (Yes—the Greeks would have fought the Greeks. Punishment for denying military service was severe, and it would have helped create this somewhat unnatural situation.) And Xerxes also called upon half of his standing army; three of the six army corps were deployed, each being made up of around 60,000 men. So, in total, Xerxes had an army of around 180,000 men at his command for the invasion of Greece.

The other thing Xerxes did to help increase his chances of success during his invasion was to construct a vast supply line for his armies. Markets and trade posts were set up along the Thracian coast to store grain and facilitate the movement of supplies needed to move such a large group of people around the Aegean Sea and down into Greece. This move showed Xerxes' prowess as a military commander, for he was willing to spend the time needed to make a proper invasion of Greece, instead of rushing into conflict and risking a swift and humiliating defeat.

His movement through Asia Minor and over into Greece was slow and gradual, and therefore not hidden from the Greeks. Word spread quickly of a massive force led by a man "more powerful than Zeus" heading their way to conquer them. Obviously fearful of this impending threat to their independence, the Greeks began to scramble to put together a defense. Since most of the Greeks who had settled in Asia Minor and Africa had already been conquered by the Persians and were in fact fighting in their armies and navies against their kinsman, often by the Persian use of the lash, the remaining independent city-states had few if any allies willing to contribute to their defense.

The northern parts of Greece, south of Macedonia and west of Delphi and Athens, were able to remain neutral, and since they had no part in the original cause of the Greco-Persian Wars (the Ionian revolts), they were not a primary concern of Xerxes and the Persians.

But all of this meant the Greeks were hopelessly alone. Threatened city-states, such as Sparta, Athens, Delphi, and Eretria attempted to form an alliance, but this was stunted by the unwillingness of the oracles to permit war against the Persians. Nearly all records of soothsayers at the time indicate that Greek priests wanted the Greek armies and leaders to abandon their land and surrender to the Persians. Even if one doesn't believe in oracles, it's no surprise this was the recommendation. The Greeks were standing alone against perhaps the largest army ever assembled.

By 480 BCE, Xerxes and his troops were marching along the Thracian coast, with his large naval fleet accompanying them and helping them cross difficult terrain wherever necessary. They moved into Macedonia and headed south toward Greece (Figure 11 shows a map of Persian troop movements during this part of the Greco-Persian Wars). Greek scouts who were captured were usually taken in and shown the immensity of the Persian army so that they could return to their leaders and report on what they saw, an attempt to solicit Greek submission before the invasion. However, this did not work, and it appeared the Greeks were going to stand up and fight for their independence, although all indications showed that they were setting up for a quick and conclusive defeat.

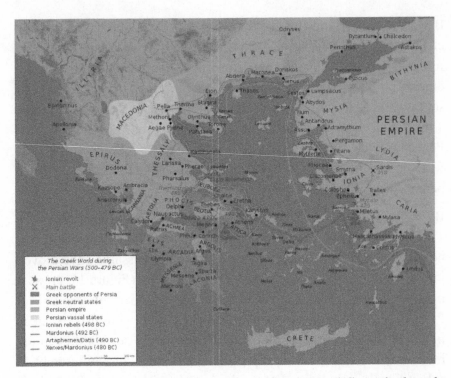

The Greek World during
the Persian Wars (500-479 BC)

- ✦ Ionian revolt
- ✗ Main battle
- ▨ Greek opponents of Persia
- ▨ Greek neutral states
- ▨ Persian empire
- ▨ Persian vassal states
- — Ionian rebels (498 BC)
- — Mardonius (492 BC)
- — Artaphernes/Datis (490 BC)
- — Xerxes/Mardonius (480 BC)

By the end of 480 BCE, Xerxes and his armies and fleets had made it to Salamis, an island just off the coast of Athens. He appeared to be in an ideal position to force the surrounding city-states to accept surrender terms, which would have left Athens all but defeated. However, Xerxes listened to his advisers and instead launched an offensive in the straits of Salamis. Ground troops were approaching from the north, and they were met by a small contingent of Greek soldiers at the Pass of Thermopylae. Here the Greeks were essentially slaughtered, although references to the battle in pop culture (the movie *300*), suggest otherwise. The Greeks were also defeated at Artemisium, despite being reinforced by those fleeing the Battle of Thermopylae. These Persian victories led to the conquest of Greek city-states such as Phocis, Boeotia, Attica, and Euboea, which gave Persia a significant stronghold into Greece, threatening Athens.

The Greek response was to engage the Persian naval fleet at the Straits of Salamis, a narrow stretch of water just off the coast of Athens. This took the Greeks out of Athens and put them on an offensive against the Persians, who were at the island of Salamis likely preparing for an invasion of Athens. This move by the Greeks gave them greater control over the conditions of engagement, which put them at an advantage. The Persians greatly outnumbered the Greeks, but attacking instead of waiting to be attacked paid off. The small space within which they had to operate proved to be a great hindrance to their success. Persian troops had trouble staying organized and keeping formation, and this meant the much smaller Athenian fleet was able to mount an attack that resulted in a decisive victory for the Greeks, dramatically reshaping the course of the war.

However, the impact of the Battle of Salamis was not felt so much in terms of the Persian military. Overall, the Persians had suffered modest defeats. And after their victories at Thermopylae and Artemisium, the army was still intact and in good position to continue its advance southward toward Athens. But what did change as a result of the Battle of Salamis was Xerxes. It was he who ordered the attack on the Athenians, meaning he had no one to blame for the loss, but immediately after the defeat, he had his Phoenician naval captains executed on grounds of cowardice. Horrified by this cruel and irrational response to what was nothing more than a normal naval defeat, the Phoenicians and Egyptians both abandoned Xerxes and returned home, drastically reducing the size of the fleet he had at his disposal and opening the door for the allied Greek city-states to launch a counteroffensive the next year, which would effectively end the Persian advance into Greece and mark the beginning of the Greek offensive into Persia.

The other major development that came from defeat at Salamis was that Xerxes, who we must remember was not particularly warlike from the beginning, left the battlefield and retreated to Sardis—the capital of Persia's Asia Minor satrap. He left Mardonius to control the army, which in other circumstances would have been a smart move, given Mardonius' record as a proven military general more adept than Xerxes. Leaving him in command would have increased

Persian chances for success, largely because Xerxes as a military leader was more of a liability than an advantage. .

The following year, 479 BCE, the Persians were still in a good position to finish their conquest. Half of the Greek city-states were under Persian control, and the allied forces did not have the numbers to beat the Persians. But there was still resistance to their rule. Greek advisers to Maradonius suggested he forgo military campaigns in favor of diplomacy, suggesting he use bribery as a means of winning the support of the Greek political elite, which would have made it much easier to win the favor of the Greek people.

However, Maradonius ignored this advice and instead chose to attack at both Platea and Mycale. But before doing this, Maradonius had taken steps to consolidate the army. Instead of relying on a massive force of conscripts taken from various parts of the empire, he sent all but one army corps home, and his remaining force was made up of only Iranians, i.e., Persians, Medes, Bactrians, and Indians, as well as Persian Immortals (a special class of professional Persian soldier which will be discussed further in Chapter 6). He believed Iranians to be stronger and more effective soldiers, and therefore felt success was more likely if he reduced the size of his force and made use of only the "best" soldiers. And he would have liked his chances even more considering he thought the Greek soldiers to be weak and ineffective, a sign of Persian military ignorance.

But the decision to attack instead of using diplomacy, along with the disregard for the ability of Greek soldiers, led to defeat at both Platea and Mycale, meaning that by the end of 479 BCE, the Persians had effectively been defeated in Greece. And as discontent began to break out in western Asia, the Persian army needed to leave Europe and attend to other matters in the empire.

There is a general consensus among historians that the Persians should have won this war. They vastly outnumbered the Greeks, and the alliance formed between the Greek city-states was weak and disorganized. Xerxes started out in the right direction by supplying his army and moving gradually into Greek territory, making sure the navy supported the army the whole way. However, some fluke defeats, followed by Xerxes' descent into madness, and then a series of military blunders by his chief commander meant the European campaign ended in defeat.

This marks an important turning point in Persian history. The Persian retreat gave the Greeks the chance to reorganize, and over the course of the next century, they would slowly come together and strengthen. This period of fortification reached a climax when the Greeks, led by Alexander the Great, eventually rode into Persia and conquered it, resulting in the fall of the Achaemenid Dynasty and the Persian Empire they controlled.

However, the implications of the Persian defeat extend much further. The Greeks would go on after this to make significant contributions to world culture in fields ranging from science and math to philosophy and the arts. However, had the Persians succeeded in wiping them off the map in the 5th century BCE, then much of this may have never happened, which would have made today's world a much different place.

The Decline of Xerxes and Persian Power

Although once considered a promising crown prince, and also a hopeful military commander, Xerxes returned from Greece a changed man. He was no longer as interested in expanding the empire, or even building upon his palace. Instead, he fell deep into harem life, leaving much of the management of his empire to his advisers and satraps.

A particularly low moment for Xerxes came when he was in Sardis after retreating from Greece: he fell in love with his brother's wife. And when she rejected his advances, he decided to marry his son to her daughter, hoping this would help him win over her favor. However, soon after, Xerxes changed his focused from his brother's wife to his son's, and these actions repulsed most of his court.

On top of this, Xerxes embarked on an aggressive taxation campaign that would have put considerable stress on the entire empire. While Persia had long since been exempt from paying taxes, the rest of the empire was not. And seeking to consolidate his power even further, he raised the tribute expectations for kingdoms across the lands he controlled.

This quickly drained much of the gold and silver from the empire, which Xerxes had melted down and stored in his palace in Persepolis. And it also helped to sow discontent throughout the empire, which the Greeks, eager to continue their resistance to Egyptian rule as well as push their influence further into Asia, were willing to fund and support through the Delian League.

The last 15 years of Xerxes' rule was relatively uneventful, and his increasing incompetence as a ruler led to his assassination in 465 BCE. He would be succeeded by his son, Artaxerxes I, who would promptly need to deal with the effects of his father's failures, which were manifesting mainly as a widespread revolt in Egypt.

The Egyptians were being supported in their attempt to rebel by the Athenians, and in an effort to try and diminish their influence in the conflict, Artaxerxes I began funding the Athenians' enemies in Greece, a move that prompted them to move their treasury and once again focus on their efforts against the Persians. However, all of this proved unsuccessful. Artaxerxes was able to quell the rebellion in Egypt, effectively ending Athenian and Delian League support of the insurrection there. The Persians continued to fight the Athenians, led by their leader Cimon, throughout Asia Minor, until the Battle of Cyprus in 450 BCE, which provided little gains to either side. Seeing that this constant war was going nowhere, Cimon and Artaxerxes I agreed to what is known as the Peace of Callias, which effectively ended the Greco-Persian Wars.

Artaxerxes I would reign in relative peace until his death in 424 BCE, at which point the monarchy would enter a period of extreme instability. Artaxerxes had only one legitimate son, Xerxes II, and he was promptly named king after the death of his father. However, days after being named king, he was killed by his illegitimate half-brother, Sogdianus, who days later was killed by his half-brother, Ochus. In an attempt to establish himself as the rightful heir to the monarchy, Ochus took the royal name Darius II. His claim was contested, and he spent most of his time putting down rebellions throughout the empire.

His death, just 12 years later, again created a chaotic situation at the head of the Persian Empire. Darius II's wife, Queen Parysatis, begged her husband to name not their eldest son, Artaxerxes II, to the throne, but rather their next oldest, Cyrus the Younger. She failed, and Artaxerxes II assumed the throne. He had his brother Cyrus the Younger arrested, and he had scheduled for his execution, although Parysatis intervened and prevented it from happening.

Artaxerxes II and Artaxerxes III: The Final Glory of the Achaemenid Empire

The ascension of Artaxerxes II in 412 BCE put an end to the turmoil that had defined the Persian Empire since the death of Xerxes in 467 BCE. He would rule for the next 45 years and help restore peace and stability to the empire. But this did not mean his reign was uneventful. In fact, it was defined once again by insurrection and revolt, and most of his military campaigns were dedicated to reestablishing his grip on power.

The first issue he had to deal with was the revolt of Egypt. This was hardly the first time the Egyptians seized the opportunity presented by a change in monarch to try and win their independence, but it was one of the first times they succeeded in doing so. Artaxerxes spent time gathering a force to try and reconquer it in 373 BCE, but this failed, and he was forced to accept that Egypt would no longer be a part of the Persian Empire.

But once again, the Greeks were beginning to antagonize the Persians. This time, however, it wasn't the Athenians but rather the Spartans who were in opposition to Persia. They had invaded Asia

Minor, the beginning point for most Greco-Persian conflicts. Yet Artaxerxes did not want to engage them directly, choosing instead to fund the Spartan's main enemy, the Athenians, who less than a century earlier had been in direct conflict with the Persians. This tied the two Greek city-states up in conflict with each other, but Artaxerxes II would shake things up by turning on his Athenian allies and making a treaty with Sparta that gave control over the cities of Ionia and Aeolis on the Anatolian coast back to the Persians.

Another revolt broke out in 372, which is known as the Revolt of the Satraps, in which provincial governors from Armenia, Cappadocia (a region in Turkey), and Phyrigia (also in Turkey) joined together to try and overthrow Artaxerxes II. This resulted in a war that ended with the satraps' defeat in 362 BCE.

Artaxerxes II was not an expansionist. While he attempted to regain control of territories lost to revolt, he was not interested in extending Persian power, and when he lost Egypt, he seemed willing to accept this defeat. However, his effectiveness in putting down the various revolts that broke out during his time as king helped bring stability and economic prosperity to the empire.

He spent a good deal of energy building up Persian cities and expanding the palaces in Susa, as well as moving his capital back to Persepolis and dedicating resources to its development. Furthermore, and this might be Artaxerxes II's most significant cultural achievement, he oversaw the expansion of Zoroastrianism, the religion that had become the official Persian religion under Artaxerxes I, and which is discussed in greater detail in Chapter 7. The shrines he built to the Zoroastrian gods and prophets are some of the more remarkable architectural accomplishments of the Persian Empire. Because of his lack of conquest and expansion, Artaxerxes II is not considered to be one of the more glorious Persian rulers. But it's clear he had a significant effect on Persian cultural development. The dynasty that came after the Achaemenids, the Parthians, traced their lineage back to Artaxerxes II to establish their legitimacy, suggesting Artaxerxes II is an important figure in the collective understanding of Persian identity. Part of this also comes from Artaxerxes II's immense family. Records indicate he had some 115 sons and as many as 350 wives.

However, Artaxerxes II's reign would eventually come to an end, and this would once again thrust the Persian Empire into a period of dramatic instability, but this time it would be unable to recover. His one final push would fail to reestablish Persian dominance, and the glory of the Achaemenids would be relegated to the annals of history.

His son, Artaxerxes III, took over as king, and as one might expect, his tenure as king started with the need to suppress the various satrapies and kingdoms who were contesting his claim to the throne. Asia Minor had been difficult to reliably control since Cyrus II first conquered Lydia back in the 7th century BCE, and this trend would continue even after 300 years of Persian influence in the region and repeated attempts to conquer and control it.

Attempting to avoid a long, costly, and likely unproductive campaign into Asia Minor, Artaxerxes III was looking for a different way to bring long-lasting peace to the region. He began diplomatically arranging a peace agreement with the Athenians, who were constantly meddling in Asia Minor due to the large presence of Greeks in the region. This treaty forced the Persians to recognize the independence of the Greek city-states in Asia Minor. Next, he moved to disband the armies of the various satrapies throughout Asia Minor, a play he hoped would help disarm the rebellious leaders in the region and prevent them from making any serious threat to Persian power.

But none of this worked, and Artaxerxes III was forced to revert to the tactics of his predecessors. Athens betrayed Artaxerxes III and sent forces to help the rebels win back Sardis, which they did. But then in 353 BCE, Artaxerxes III launched a full-scale campaign through Asia Minor which was successful in disbanding the rebellious armies and securing Persian control in the region.

Shortly after his success in Asia Minor, Artaxerxes III began to set his sights on Egypt, the territory his father had lost and failed to regain. But almost as soon as Artaxerxes III entered Egypt and engaged the Egyptians, rebellion broke out again in Asia Minor, which this time the Egyptians supported. Yet Artaxerxes III continued into Egypt until he was defeated, and by the time this happened, Phoenicia, Asia Minor, and now Cyprus were in full-scale revolt. An attempt to quell the rebellion in Cyprus failed, and the Persians were soon driven out of Phoenicia, bringing the Persian Empire to its smallest area since Cyrus II and Cambyses first established Persian dominance throughout western Asia.

In 343 BCE, Artaxerxes III once again turned his attention back to Egypt, and this time he was successful in bringing the Egyptian king into submission. Afterward, he installed a reign of terror that involved the burning of religious and cultural buildings, and anyone caught practicing Egyptian religions was persecuted and often executed. The idea was to try and discourage the Egyptians from ever revolting again, and it had the additional effect of stopping other regions in the Persian Empire from revolting; victory over Egypt seemed to be enough for these rebellious groups to see that Artaxerxes III still commanded a powerful army that should not be challenged. However, Macedon, led by Phillip III of Macedon, was gaining considerable power on the other side of the Aegean Sea, and their rise meant Persia's days as western Asia's superpower were limited.

During these final stages of campaigning, Artaxerxes III appointed a man named Bagoas to be one of his highest-ranking advisers, but this move would prove to be ill-fated, as Bagoas had his own ambitions and ended up poisoning Artaxerxes III with the help of a physician. Artaxerxes III died in 338 BCE.

The End of The Achaemenid Dynasty

Artaxerxes IV succeeded Artaxerxes III, but before he was able to do anything, he too was poisoned by Bagoas, who then moved to place Artaxerxes IV's nephew, Darius III, on the throne. Shortly after this happened, Darius III, aware of Bagoas' actions, forced him to take poison. Egypt, once again, revolted, and Darius III had to send troops to quell the rebellion.

But at this point, it did not really matter who was king of Persia or if the Egyptians had been subdued. Alexander III of Macedon, who is known to the rest of the world as Alexander the Great, had taken his large, battled-hardened army into Asia Minor during 334 BCE. He quickly defeated the Persian armies at Granicus in 334, Issus in 333, and Gaugamela in 331. He then followed up these victories by attacking Susa and the Persian capital, Persepolis, both of which surrendered in 330 BCE.

Darius III had run to Ecbatana and then continued on to Bactria, where he was murdered by the Bactrian satrap, Bessus, who then declared himself Artaxerxes V, king of Persia. But this lasted for almost no time at all. Alexander and his armies marched into Bactria, found Bessus, or Artaxerxes V, and put him on trial in Persian court, where he was sentenced to be executed.

Some scholars consider Alexander the Great to be the "last of the Achaemenids," largely because he kept most of the Persian political apparatus intact after his conquest. However, he was not Persian and had no claim to the Persian throne. Yet his willingness to leave administration of the empire the way it was can in part be attributed to his relatively successful rule over western Asia.

When Alexander the Great died in 323 BCE, his now massive empire, which extended from Greece all the way to the Indus River, was divided among his generals with the largest territory, the one in which the Iranian plateau was located, being given to Seleucus I

Nicator, who would govern over the territory once known as the Persian Empire but that was now understood as the Seleucid Empire.

Conclusion

As is the case with most ancient empires, the demise of the Persian Empire under the Achaemenid Dynasty seems to have occurred quickly. However, when looking more closely at the events that led up to its downfall, it's easy to see how precarious Persia's grip on power really was, and it's also easy to see how the complex geopolitical situation of Mesopotamia and abroad made it difficult to maintain an empire of that size for too long.

But this is not meant to discount the accomplishments of the Achaemenid Dynasty. In a matter of just 300 years, it went from being the leader of an obscure Persian tribe on the Iranian plateau to being one of the largest and most formidable empires in the history of the ancient world.

However, the region Persia controlled was simply too large, too diverse, and subjected to too many influences for them to hope to hold onto power forever. So even though the Persian military at the time was one of the strongest seen to date, the competing political powers within the state, combined with the frequent revolts from conquered territories and overly ambitious attempts at expansion into Europe started by Darius I and continued by Xerxes, all contributed to the eventual downfall of the Persian Empire under the Achaemenid Dynasty. But this would not be the end of Persian history. Within a few hundred years of Alexander the Great's conquest of Persia, a new dynasty, which would trace its roots back to the Achaemenids but that would be known as the Parthians, would merge and restore Iranians to power in Persia and across western Asia.

Chapter 5 – Life in Ancient Persia

Almost as soon as Persia became an empire under the Achaemenid Dynasty, it also became a large, diverse nation. Its borders stretched from Egypt to Turkey, parts of Greece, Armenia, Iraq, Iran, Arabia, Afghanistan, Uzbekistan, and even into India, and nearly all the lands in between, which included powerful and influential cultures such as the Phoenicians, the Jews, the Medes, the Babylonians, and many more. As a result, it's impossible to describe Persia as a unified society with its own distinct cultural norms.

Instead, it's better to think of it as a loose coalition of different cultures, many of which were brought together by force, but that remained connected through Persia's highly-developed, centralized form of political organization that was set up by Darius I (see Chapter 3). Nevertheless, we can still paint a picture of what life might have been like for the people living in the Persian Empire.

The Persians themselves, who resided in Persis, which is in the modern country of Iran, would have been at the center of the empire. However, due to its lack of arable land and harsh terrain, Persia itself was far from the most developed part of the empire. In fact, before the Persian tribes were unified under Cyrus II, Iran was barely settled. It was instead inhabited mostly by nomadic tribes, which would have put the Persians far behind their neighbors in Mesopotamia in terms of urban development and social advancement.

Because of Iran's difficult topography, good, fertile land was scarce, which led to the development of a landowning class that would serve as the nobility during the Persian Empire. Before the birth of the empire and during its existence, Persia would have been a feudal society, meaning peasants would have been expected to pay rent to a landowner in exchange for the right to work the land, and some of the fruits of their labor would have been paid back to the landowner as a tax.

However, as the empire grew and expanded, the Persian people living in Persia would have likely experienced a dramatic improvement in their quality of life. First, the completion of the Royal Road by Darius I connected Sardis in Asia Minor with Susa and Ecbatana, as well as other cities throughout Media and Bactria. This would have brought new goods from afar into Persia, and it would have made it easier for them to trade with other parts of the empire. Furthermore, Persia itself was exempt from paying imperial taxes and tributes, which would have significantly reduced the imperial burden on the Persian people.

Another thing that would have contributed to the Persian people's relatively high standard of living would have been the exit of the landowning class. Once Cyrus II conquered Babylon and it was fortified by Darius I, much of the landowning class would have moved out of Persia into Babylon and Mesopotamia. Farmland was far better and more bountiful in the Fertile Crescent, meaning it would have been easier for them to increase their wealth. The feudal system remained, but it's likely its burden was not as heavy as compared to what would have happened had the Persian elite elected to stay in the Iranian plateau.

Life in Persia also would have been relatively peaceful. War did not reach the homeland until Alexander the Great began conquering western Asia. But this does not mean the Persian people were unfamiliar with war. Military service was required, and many men would spend much of their lives away from home fighting in the different theaters around the empire. However, Persian use of mercenaries, conscripts, and slaves in their armies would have reduced the need for Persian soldiers, although most Persian kings considered their kinsman to be naturally better fighters. A more detailed description of the Persian military is given in Chapter 6.

Like all pre-modern societies, Persia was a largely agrarian culture. Inside Persia itself, livestock would have been the primary produce, largely because scarce arable land made it hard to produce a surplus of agricultural goods. However, through trade with the provinces throughout the empire, Persians would have had access to many of the goods enjoyed in Mesopotamia and abroad, including wheat and barley. It's difficult to ascertain exactly how well people lived, largely because of a lack of records. But it's reasonable to believe the peasantry lived in what would today be considered rural poverty. Yet the absence of military conquest and the availability of goods through trade would have brought significant improvements to the peasantry's quality of life.

Elsewhere in the empire, the presence of the Persian Empire would have brought considerable prosperity for several reasons. First, the construction of the Royal Road made it much easier for merchants to travel across western Asia and trade with one another. Also, the centralized bureaucracy of the Persian Empire made it easy for people from different cultural, linguistic, and ethnic backgrounds to engage with each other economically

Another thing that contributed to the economic prosperity of the Persian Empire was the introduction of currency. Cyrus II first introduced gold coins to the empire, but it was Darius I who would expand upon the practice by standardizing a gold coin. It weighed 8.4 kilograms, and it was the equivalent of 20 silver coins. Currency was already in use in some form or another throughout the empire, particularly in the Greek city-states that were located in Asia Minor, but this standardization would have made it much easier for different parts of the empire to trade with one another. However, the Persian monarchs, especially starting with Xerxes, had a propensity to hoard gold and silver. This would have slowed the circulation of coinage around the empire, which would have reduced the importance of currency. But even so, this development was rather significant to the economic development of the region.

The last major reason the Persian Empire would have helped usher in a period of relative economic stability and prosperity was Darius I's policy of tolerance and acceptance. Because he did not attempt to persecute people based on their religion and culture, most people would have lived in relative peace throughout the time of Persian dominance. Of course, rebellions and insurrections were common throughout the empire, and war was constant. But this would have been limited to the regions on the periphery. The rest of the empire would have enjoyed considerable stability that allowed for a growth in wealth.

The Persians also helped usher in the adoption of Aramaic as the lingua franca of the empire. Although one would have encountered a different language in almost every corner of the empire, the establishment of Aramaic, which was a Semitic language used mostly in cities of modern Syria, as the official language of the empire gave the region a *lingu franca* to use in law and business. Part of the reason this language was chosen was because it was highly standardized and uniform, meaning it was easier to learn than other languages in the region. Some scholars have called Aramaic the Persian Empire's official language, but this is incorrect, as it would have likely only been spoken outside its traditional regions to conduct business, legal, and government affairs. Nonetheless, the use of a common language would have made it far easier for the many different peoples of the Persian Empire to communicate and interact with one another, something that helped to strengthen Persian imperial power.

Overall, life in the Persian Empire would not have been all that different than life in many of the other ancient civilizations of this part of the world. Daily life would have consisted of farming, praying to the gods, military training and service, or engaging in whichever trade or craft you had been trained to perform. The major changes that took place would have been in the political and bureaucratic arrangements of the empire. But some of these changes would have helped usher in a higher quality of life and increased connectivity between many different cultures. However, these improvements and advancements would come as a result of the Persian monarchy's conquests and expansion, meaning war would have been a central part of life for most of the people living during the time of the Persian Empire.

Chapter 6 – The Persian Military

Seizing and holding onto power in the ancient world could not be done without a large, strong, and effective military. The Assyrians, who preceded the Persians as western Asia's hegemon, had developed a military machine that would strike fear in the hearts of nearly all its neighbors, moving many kingdoms to submit merely out of fear of what could happen to them should they be subjected to an Assyrian invasion.

The Persians were no different. While the Assyrians might go down in history as one of the most ruthless military cultures to have ever walked the Earth, the Persians were able to create and sustain a large military that would be the source of their power throughout the entire duration of the Achaemenid Dynasty. The core of the Persian army was made up of Persians themselves, but the Achaemenids also made use of many other groups of people to help them sustain their large armies and maintain control over their empire.

The Persian Immortals

This particular rank of Persian soldiers was considered to be one of the most powerful forces in all of western Asia and abroad, and they have gone down in history as one of the world's most famous military units. They were deemed "immortal" because by law the size of the force was never allowed to drop below 10,000. This meant that, in theory, as soon as a Persian soldier died, he would immediately be replaced by another, preventing any enemy from doing real damage to the Persian military.

To fill these ranks, the Persian monarchs drew from their own people; Persians were not required to pay taxes and tribute to the crown, but they were expected to lay down their lives and fight for their king no questions asked. However, it was also common to find Medes and Elamites among the ranks of the Immortals, as these three civilizations were closely aligned both culturally and politically. Once selected, they would be sent to Susa to train and then join the ranks of the Immortals wherever they were in the empire at the time. This created a situation where the Persian army had a constant flow of reinforcements, helping to make it more effective and better able to wage long military campaigns against foreign enemies.

Persian Immortals were given special treatment. They were dressed well, and their uniforms often featured highly-decorative gold ornaments. And when these soldiers traveled, they were permitted to take servants and concubines with them, and they were often served special food on camels or other baggage animals. To add to their grandeur and also to try and intimidate enemy forces, Persian Immortals were all dressed the same. Their heads were shaved, and their short beards were curled. Golf bracelets drooped over their arms, and their spears were made with silver blades that would have helped prove they were indeed a member of the 10,000 Immortals. They would have also had a bow and a quiver thrown over their shoulder, but an Immortal would not have been permitted to carry any other weapon besides the spear and bow.

Satrapal Armies

While the Immortals would have represented the highest ranks of the Persian military, 10,000 men would not have been nearly enough to secure the empire and tend to its many foes both near and far—remember Xerxes invaded Greece with a force of over 150,000 men and the naval fleets of three very powerful kingdoms.

In an attempt to maintain control over the different regions of the empire, the Persian kings required each satrap to contribute a certain number of troops. The king would appoint a military commander to direct the satrapal armies, and then each regional leader would be responsible for meeting the quotas mandated by the king and his commanders, a number that would depend heavily on the campaign being conducted and the types of soldiers a satrap could offer. For example, the Egyptians and Phoenicians were relied upon heavily for their navies, whereas the Persians drew from their Median, Bactrian, and Indian provinces for ground soldiers.

Unlike the Immortals, there would have been little to no uniformity in terms of what the satrapal armies would have worn. Each group would have adorned whatever clothing was the norm for soldiers from their region, and this oftentimes made it difficult for enemies to know they were even fighting Persians. Furthermore, this forced conscription of satrapal populations meant that although the Persian army was large, it was made up mostly of people who had been forced into service. As a result, depending on the political situation of the time, the effectiveness of these forces would vary. For example, the Egyptians and Phoenicians were committed to helping Xerxes with his invasion of Greece until he decided to ruthlessly execute Phoenician commanders. They responded by leaving Greece and deserting Xerxes in the middle of his campaign to invade Europe, something that significantly hurt his chances at victory.

Dependence on these satrapal armies set up an interesting conundrum that is commonly seen in civilizations across the ancient world. On the one hand, Persia needed to conquer and expand its territorial control so as to be able to recruit an army large enough to maintain its control over conquered territories. It should come as no surprise then that many of the satrapies, especially those located on the periphery of the empire, were subjected to constant warfare. On the other hand, other kings in the region, attempting to regain autonomy after being conquered, would have competed for the loyalties of these same people, for this is how they would stock their armies and succeed as king. This meant that people were constantly changing allegiances and that it would have been difficult to rely solely on the satrapies for filling the ranks of the Persian armies. .

Mercenaries and Other Armies

In addition to the Immortals and satrapal armies, the Persians also relied heavily on mercenaries, especially for their naval units. They also made widespread use of slave armies, taking people from conquered lands and forcing them into military service. Their military units were formed based on need and also the relationship a satrap had with the king. Military units might be granted some degree of autonomy, or they might be absorbed into the larger Persian army. For example, after one of the initial Babylonian revolts, the region was annexed and added to the satrap of Assyria. From that moment on, no mention of Babylonian troops exists. They likely would not have been trusted enough to operate on their own, and their status would have been relegated to that of a slave.

Persian military might was one of the main reasons why it was able to gain such considerable territory and power over such a short period of time. The initial successes of Cyrus II gave future kings the notion that Persian soldiers were stronger and more capable than any other group within the empire. This gave way to the formation of the Persian Immortals, which would be the most terrifying and effective military force during the time period when the Persians controlled all the lands from Egypt to India.

Chapter 7 – Zoroastrianism: Persia's Religion

Similar to other ancient civilizations, religion played an important role in both the lives of commoners as well as leaders in the Persian Empire. But unlike the previous empires of western Asia, namely Sumeria, Assyria, and Babylon, the Persians were monotheistic. They practiced a religion known as Zoroastrianism, which is named after its chief prophet, Zoroaster, sometimes known as Zarathustra. Its origins trace back to the second millennium BCE, which makes it one of the oldest monotheistic religions in human history. It is still practiced today, but starting with the Arab invasion of Persia in the 7th century CE, Islam began to spread across the Iranian plateau. Later on, the Iranian Revolution, which took place in the 20th century, put Zoroastrianism further into the background of Persian/Iranian culture, but it remains prominent and is even seeing a revival as modern Iranians seek to push back from the Islamic theocracy that dominates their country's politics.

The Founding of Zoroastrianism

The first mention of Zoroastrianism as an organized religion appear in the 5th century when the Greek historian Herodotus, often called the father of history, wrote *The Histories*, which is a detailed account of the many different cultures and civilizations that existed and interacted with one another across western Asia and southern Europe.

However, many historians believe the core beliefs and practices of Zoroastrianism can trace their roots back to Indo-Iranian customs that became popular starting c. 2500 BCE. Yet it's likely that somewhere in between is when it took shape as the religion that would eventually become a defining characteristic of Persian culture. It's believed that Zoroaster, who is considered a prophet in the religion but who was most likely a religious reformer, began spreading his version of the faith in the 10th century BCE.

Little by little, the teachings of Zoroaster penetrated the collective psyche of the Persian people, and they even had an influence in the development of other religious traditions, such as Zurvanism, the main religion of the Magi, a tribe which held considerable influence at the Median courts. It's believed that the initial spread of Zoroastrianism was actually meant to help limit the power of this particular group after Cyrus the Great was able to bring the Persian and Median kingdoms together, laying the foundation for what would become the great Persian Empire.

But it would not be accurate to say that Cyrus II and his immediate successors, such as Cambyses and Darius I, were Zoroastrians themselves. At the time, many Persians believed in the Zoroastrian deity, Ahura Mazda, but this did not mean they were followers of Zoroaster and his teachings. But as the Persian Empire expanded, so would the influence of Zoroastrianism on its people, resulting in it eventually becoming the main religion of Persia under Artaxerxes II.

Zoroastrian Beliefs

First and foremost, Zoroastrianism is a monotheistic religion, meaning it believes in only one god, Ahura Mazda, which translates from Old Iranian and Persian into Wise Lord. Ahura literally means "being," whereas Mazda means "mind." Zoroaster taught this distinction so as to highlight the concept of duality, and he also made sure to refer to one as masculine and one as feminine, likely an attempt to not depict Ahura Mazda as a human. Furthermore, Zoroaster taught that Ahura Mazda was almighty, but not omnipotent, an important distinction and one that not many religions of the time made, especially those based in polytheism.

One of the defining characteristics of Zoroastrianism is the significance it places on duality. Specifically, it depicts the world as being locked in a struggle between good and evil, and that the end of times will coincide with a final triumph of good. Ahura Mazda manifests through the Spenta Mainyu, which are divine entities. The term literally translates to divine holys. Through these entities, Ahura Mazda serves as a benevolent "father" responsible for overcoming the influence of Druj, which means falsehood or deceit. There is no evil in Ahura Mazda, and his primary responsibility to humanity is to help it overcome the forces of evil trying to push it toward destruction.

The pillars of Zoroastrianism are: 1) Humata, Hukhta, Huvarshta, which translate to Good Thoughts, Good Words, Good Deeds; 2) There is only one path, the path of Truth; and 3) Do the right thing because it's right, and then you will see rewards later.

This belief in an almighty deity fighting to spread good and defeat evil represents a significant development as compared to early Iranian religions, which trace back to Aryan customs that defined no good or deity, and instead thought the world was governed by different evil spirits and demons. Another interesting aspect of Zoroastrianism is that it asks its followers to protect nature, specifically outlining the need to maintain earth, air, wind, and water, which has led many theologians to declare Zoroastrianism the world's first ecological religion, although this title has been contested by some.

However, no matter which way one looks at it, Zoroastrianism was a peaceful religion. Unlike the religions of other ancient civilizations, such as Assyria or Babylon, it did not preach warfare as a necessary means for existence and survival. This belief could help explain why Persian kings were rarely if ever interested in changing the religious customs practiced by those they conquered; persecution typically only took place when it was politically necessary.

Furthermore, some of the principal ideas in Zoroastrian teachings, such as the idea of a messiah, judgment after death, the idea of heaven and hell, and free will, helped to shape other religious traditions, most notably Second Temple Judaism, Gnosticism, Christianity, and Islam. Zoroastrianism remained the principal religion of the Persian people until the Arabs invaded in the 7th century CE. From that point on, Islam was the primary religion of the region, and beyond this point in history, Zoroastrianism was often persecuted.

Today, there are estimated to be some 200,000 practices of Zoroastrianism scattered throughout Iran and India. And while its significance diminished significantly after the Arab invasion of Persia, it had a significant effect on the cultural development of Persia and of western Asia as a whole.

Chapter 8 – Later Persian Dynasties: The Parthian Empire to the Qajar Dynasty

After the fall of Susa and Persepolis to Alexander the Great in 330 BCE, the Achaemenid Dynasty fell. The Persian Empire was now a part of Alexander's vast dominion, and when he died, it was left in the hands of one of his generals, Seluceus I Nicator, who formed the Seleucid Empire, which consisted of the territories on the Iranian plateau and into Media and parts of Mesopotamia, although it would never reach even a semblance of the size and glory of Persia under the Achaemenids. The Persians were denied the ability to govern their own homeland for just a little over 100 years after being conquered by Alexander.

However, just because the Achaemenids fell from power, this did not signal the end of the Persians. In fact, using a broad lens of history, it was really just the beginning. Different Persian dynasties would emerge after the fall of the Seleucid Empire, and this would help carry the Persian Empire well into the modern era. It fell once again in the 19th century under the Qajar Dynasty, and this paved the way for the formation of the country of Iran.

These different dynasties that came after the Achaemenids experienced varying levels of success. For example, the Sassanian Empire, which was formed in 224 CE, lasted more than 400 years, whereas the Afsharid Dynasty, formed in 1501 CE, was on this earth for just 60 years, existing only long enough for there to be just a few kings.

Each one of these dynasties should really be studied on their own. Like the Achaemenids, they each have a rich history of conquest and consolidation, and each one made their own specific contributions to both Persian history and culture. However, looking at the major accomplishments of each one offers some perspective on how Persia has shaped the course of world history, and how it has contributed to the forming of the world in which we now live.

The Parthian Empire (247 BCE-224 CE)

The Seleucid Empire would last no more than 100 years before the Persians, starting with the Parthian Dynasty and ending with the Sassanian Dynasty, were able to retake control of their homeland, and once they did, they would succeed in holding onto it for the next 600 years.

This successor to the Achaemenids is referred to as the Parthian Empire largely because of how it came into existence. King Arsaces I of Parthia, who lead the local Parni tribe, rose up and seized the region of Parthia, which is in northeastern Iran, sometime in the mid-3rd century BCE. Later on, Parthian historians would write 247 BCE as the exact year the Parthian Empire was founded, although it's uncertain why this date was chosen as historical records do not produce evidence of any significant events during this year that could be associated with the formation of the empire. This could be because at the time Parthia was in open rebellion to Seleucid rule. It's likely Arsaces I's seizure of the territory was contested and he needed to spend a great deal of time securing the land he had just won back from the empire's central authorities.

Arsaces I's success, though, stopped there. He spent most of his reign defending himself from the region's previous imperial rulers as they attempted to take back the territory they had lost. However, they were unsuccessful, and the Parthian-led Persians were able to maintain their independence despite repeated advances from the Seleucids. It wasn't until Mithridates I came to power in c. 171 BCE that the Parthians would begin to chip away at the Seleucid Empire and establish themselves as a power in the region, once again making Persia an important political player in western Asia.

Mithridates I managed to conquer Media and Mesopotamia, which would have reduced the Seleucid Empire to not much more than the territory in what we would today call southern Iran. This all but obliterated the Seleucid Empire from history, and it once again brought Iranians to power in the Iranian plateau, which would last until the Arabs invaded in the 7th century, still some 700 years away.

However, while the Parthian Empire was able to annex a relatively large territory in western Asia, it would never match what the Achaemenids did in terms of the amount of territory they controlled and their influence over it. For example, while the Achaemenids installed a highly-centralized system of government that depended on king-appointed satraps, the Parthians relied much more heavily on local leadership. Instead of conquering, they would attempt to negotiate tribute relationships from surrounding kings, making them their vassals and easing the burden of governance that often comes with having a large empire.

The other factor limiting the expansion of the Parthians was the competition they faced for control of western Asia. Far to the west, the Roman Republic had become quite powerful and had begun to try to expand its influence in and around Iran. And in the Far East, the Chinese under the Han Dynasty were moving westward to try and expand their influence and establish trade relations. The

Parthians would never engage directly with the Chinese, largely because the eastern provinces were well defended by the kings in that area, but they would actively compete with the Romans. For example, both empires wanted to make the king of Armenia their vassal, and this led to some tense moments between the once-great Persians and the rising Romans. The Romans and Parthians also fought directly in different parts of west Asia as the Romans continued to flex their imperial muscles around the world.

But perhaps the most significant accomplishment of the Parthian Empire were the trade relations it was able to establish. Most importantly, it helped connect the Chinese Silk Road to western Asia, which made it much easier for Chinese goods to be imported into Europe. For example, the Romans bought considerable amounts of silk—its largest import—as well as pearls and other luxury goods. In return, the Chinese bought dyes and spices as well as other Middle Eastern foods. Because Persia lies strategically in the middle of these two influential regions of the world, they were able to impose duties on trade between Rome and China, enriching the empire and helping it establish itself as a significant player in western Asian politics, as well as the development of world history.

Given the time period in which the Parthian Empire existed, it shouldn't be surprising that its downfall was a direct result of the expansion of the Roman Empire. Peace treaties were frequently made and then broken, and the Persians were able to maintain autonomy largely because the Romans were hesitant to extend themselves too far to the east and deplete their military resources. However, the Romans did not capture the Parthian kings. Instead, they made slow advances into Mesopotamia, ensuring the border was fortified before continuing. For most of the time the two kingdoms coexisted, the border between the two was typically somewhere around the Tigris River.

One attempt at invasion was made by the Roman emperor Trajan (c. 100 CE), who succeeded in capturing the Persian city of Susa, one of the most important Persian cities under the Achaemenids. But this conquest did not last long as the Babylonians revolted and pushed the Romans back further west into Mesopotamia. The Romans would never again try to expand that far east, but the results of this invasion would shake the Parthian Empire at its core and trigger its fall from power.

Internal strife between the various rulers with Persia significantly weakened the Parthian grip on power, and the near-constant war with Rome also put considerable strain on their military, leaving the Parthians open to attack, which came in 224 CE when Ardashir I of Persis (which would have been the center of the Achaemenid Dynasty but that had been reduced to a province under the Parthians. It was not a capital though; the Parthians set their capitals in northeastern Iran) revolted against the Parthian Dynasty and began subjugating territories. He eventually engaged with the Parthians at the Battle of Hormozdgan in 224 CE, which Ardashir I won. This brought an end to the Parthian Empire and gave birth to the next age of Persia: the Sassanian Empire. Figure 12 shows the extent of the Parthian Empire when it was at its peak.

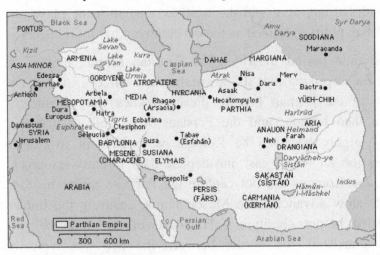

The Sassanian Empire (224 AC-651 CE)

In comparison to the Achaemenid dynasty and empire, the Parthians were much smaller and much less powerful. This is in part because of the constant competition they faced from their powerful neighbors, such as Rome. However, after the fall of the Parthian Empire, the Sassanian Empire was born, and it would last for some 400 years. It would significantly expand on the territory controlled by Persia, and it would be the last Persian Empire before the rise of Islam.

The ascension of Ardashir I was not uncontested. Rebellion broke out across the empire, and the Romans intensified their hostilities once they saw the internal struggles of the Parthians, hoping to capitalize on this to help bring the Parthians fully under Roman control. However, Ardashir I, as well as his son, Shapur I, managed to successfully campaign around the empire to put these rebellions down, and they also managed to defeat the Romans to the west, pushing the conflict back toward the Mediterranean and the Caucuses.

Rebellions continued, but by c. 300 CE, the Sassanians were firmly entrenched as the new Persian monarchs. The split of the Roman Empire meant their new opponent would be the Eastern Roman Empire, also known as the Byzantine Empire. The Sassanian Empire was constantly warring with this powerful western neighbor, and it even laid siege to Constantinople. But neither side was ever able to conquer the other, and in the end, the resource drain and political strife caused by war would prove to be the Sassanians' downfall.

However, although the Sassanian Empire was not as territorially large as the Achaemenid Empire (see Figure 13), it in many ways restored the glory of the Persian Empire and also helped establish the Persians as one of the more powerful forces in the region.

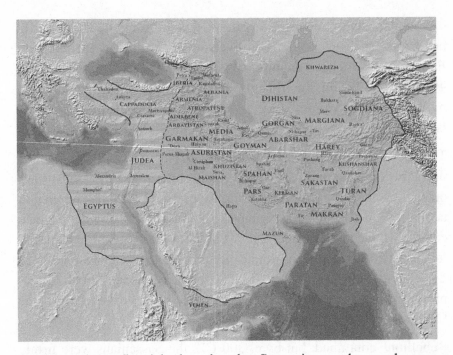

Persian culture flourished under the Sassanians, who made many contributions to the development of the region. Most specifically, the Sassanians were well known for their art, and paintings, sculptures, and decorative textiles were commissioned and traded all over the empire. Many scholars consider Sassanian art to be the predecessor to Muslim art, which would become one of the most well-known styles in all the world as Islam grew in prominence throughout the 1st millennia CE.

Part of the success of Persia under the Sassanians was that the Sassanian kings returned to the form of centralized government implemented by the Achaemenids. Unlike the Parthians, who elected instead to rely on local kings and rulers to help them enforce their rule, the Sassanians used satraps and appointed provincial governors directly, using the intricate roads system built throughout Mesopotamia and central Asia to move troops and give orders about how to best manage the empire. This helped the Sassanians become far more powerful and therefore far more influential than the Parthians.

A short description of the accomplishments of the Sassanian Empire does not do justice to its significance. But what is important to remember is that the formation of the Parthian Dynasty and then the Sassanian Dynasty is a big reason why Persian culture is still around and prominent today. Many ancient civilizations came and went, Assyria and Babylon, for example, often being absorbed by much larger powers. The Achaemenids put Persia on the map, but the almost 1,000 years of Parthian and Sassanian rule helped entrench the Persians as key contributors to the development of world culture.

And if we stop to consider that the next 900 years would see no Persian rule—the Arabs invaded and included Persia in its caliphate—the cultural achievements of the early Persian Empires can be considered even more remarkable. They had managed to become so influential in the region that even though their cultural norms were repressed—Zoroastrianism declined significantly under the Arabs—they are able to remain relevant even to this day, which is just further proof that the Persian Empire and people are some of the most important to the formation of our modern world.

The Safavid Dynasty (1501-1736 CE)

In a short period of just five years in the middle of the 7th century, the Sassanian Empire fell. Muslim armies invaded, and capitalizing on the already existing decline of the empire, were able to bring it down in c. 651. This marked the beginning of a dramatic transformation in Persian history and culture. Zoroastrianism began to decline, and Islam became the dominant religion of the time. But much like Roman/Latin culture did not disappear after the fall of Rome, Persian culture had developed to the point where it could continue growing despite the fact that Persians could not claim themselves as part of an independent nation. Still, this period of time would have a dramatic influence on Persian/Iranian history, and it would also have a large impact on the shaping of the modern world.

However, the Persians were far from gone. It took nearly 900 years, but by 1501 CE, Persia had managed to gain its independence, and the Safavid Dynasty rose to power, a group of rulers who would play a significant role in the formation of today's Iran, both in terms of territory as well as culture.

In 1501, political unrest in the region left Persia essentially without a ruler, and Shah Ismail I, whose background is disputed although he and his descendants would claim they shared lineage with the prophet Mohammad, rose to power and established the Safavid Dynasty. Little by little he was able to win over the various cities on the Iranian plateau, ending his conquest by driving the Uzbeks out of Iranian territory and also fortifying the border with the Ottoman Empire, which was western Asia's greatest power at the time. Figure 14 shows the extent of the Persian Empire under the Safavids, and it also shows the modern borders of the various countries in the region. The Safavids controlled more territory than what is considered Iran today, but the Safavid Dynasty's ability to secure these borders is partly the reason why it is considered the founder of modern Iran.

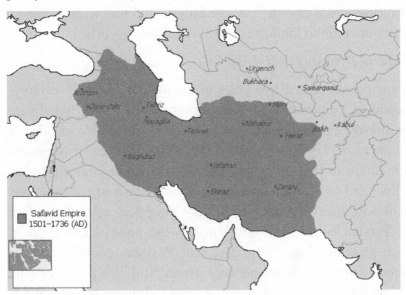

The defining characteristic of the Safavid Dynasty was the shah (king) and his power. Along with the Mughal Empire in India and the Ottoman Empire in Turkey, the Safavid Empire is one of the Gunpowder Empires, a term used to describe civilizations that were able to establish strong, militaristic states by monopolizing the use of gunpowder weapons, specifically artillery and muskets.

And while the shah ruled with absolute supremacy, there is still evidence of some democratic principles and institutions. For example, the Persian bureaucracy was large and advanced, and Persian government officials were trained to record nearly all the actions of their departments. Both of these tactics had the *de facto* effect of limiting the power of the shah, although he had complete control over the military. This concept of highly-centralized yet efficient and effective bureaucracy was a defining characteristic of Persian culture, and it traced its roots all the way back to the policies of Darius I, the third emperor of the Achaemenid Dynasty.

This strong military rule is in part the reason we have a country of Iran today. It allowed the Persians to reassert themselves as an integral part of the overland trade routes between the European powers and Eastern empires, mainly those located in China and India. By being able to secure its borders and also effectively ward off attacks by nomadic tribes and other imperial hopefuls, the shahs of the Safavid Dynasty managed to establish Persia as a powerful force in the region, something that would continue until this very day.

But perhaps the most significant contribution to Persian/Iranian culture made by the Safavids was the adoption and spread of the Shi'a branch of Islam. However, this was done in less than ethical ways. When Shah Ismail I came to power in the early 1500s, he turned his back on an old tradition of religious tolerance by the Persian kings and made Shi'a Islam the official religion of the empire, making conversion mandatory. The Sunni population, which was rather large in Persia at the time, that did not convert was either exiled or killed, and the Sunni Ulema, the priesthood, was heavily persecuted. This decision would turn out to have a dramatic effect on the course of world history. The Sunni-Shi'a conflict is one of the modern world's most significant, and it has its roots in the Safavid decision to make Shi'a Islam its official religion and scorn believers of all other faiths.

The decline of the Safavid Dynasty falls into line with the broader historical trend of European influence in other parts of the world. While wars with neighboring states depleted the resources of the Safavid Dynasty and weakened its grip on power, it was the entrance of the Dutch East India Company, as well as the British navy, that would have a significant role in bringing about the decline of the Persian Empire under the Safavids.

This entrance of the Dutch East India Company gave Europeans a monopoly over trade in the region, and they blocked non-sanctioned overseas trade routes between Iran and the rest of Asia, which slowly depleted the Persian/Iranian government of many of its resources. As a result, the Safavid Dynasty collapsed on itself, and by the early 1700s, it was under heavy attack. Different tribal and ethnic groups wreaked havoc on its borders, and the Russians and Ottomans took this moment of weakness as their opportunity to seize control of Persia, which they did. By 1724, the Safavid Dynasty was no more, and Persia was divided between the Russians and the Ottomans, bringing an end to Persian independence for the time.

The Qajar Dynasty (1789-1925)

Attempts in the mid-18th century to reestablish Persian independence failed, and it wasn't until the end of the century, with the rise of the Qajar Dynasty, that Persia would once again be able to flex its muscles as a free and independent nation. This is considered to be the last dynasty of Persia. Its fall coincided with the outbreak of World War II, and pressures from other countries as well as its own people forced it to accept a constitutional monarchy for the last 20 years of its rule. Shahs would continue to rule Iran until the Iranian Revolution in 1977, and the Qajar family still exists today, although it has no claim to rule in Iran.

The Qajar Dynasty sprung into resistance under Shah Mohammad Khan Qajar, which ended the brief Afsharid Dynasty (the aforementioned attempt to establish a Persian monarch after the fall of the Safavids). And as soon as he secured control over Iran, he immediately set his sights on the Caucuses, hoping to regain territories lost over the previous few centuries. Initial successes were followed by crushing defeats as the Russians moved against the Qajars and were able to take the territories making up modern-day Georgia, Azerbaijan, and Armenia.

These defeats led to the drawing of the Iranian borders we know today. And the Qajar Dynasty is considered responsible for the "modernization" of Iran. They built Iran's, and the Middle East's, first university, the Dar ul-Funun in Tehran in 1851. Furthermore, the Qajars ushered in Western technologies that led to the country's industrialization, and in the 20th century, they began trading fossil fuels to the rest of the world; to this day, Iran is a member of OPEC (Organization of the Oil Producing Countries), and it has the world's largest supply of natural gas.

Perhaps the most defining characteristic of the Qajar Dynasty was its submission to foreign powers. The British were becoming increasingly involved in the affairs of the Middle East, and various arrangements made by Qajar kings with British trading companies resulted in the majority of Iranian trade being handled by the British themselves. These developments led the Iranian people to feel as though their leaders were bound to foreign powers, and this was one of the driving forces behind the push for reform that occurred at the beginning of the 20th century.

It was this reform that would bring more democracy to the region than it had ever seen before. The country was in financial ruin, and the clergy and merchant classes demanded the shah cede powers so that others could manage the affairs of the country and put it in a better position for success. Protests broke out across Iran at the beginning of 1906, and by the end of the year, a constitution had been drawn up and ratified that established a parliament, limited royal power, and required the shah to get confirmation from the parliament for cabinet appointments.

This move appeared to start a process of democratic transition, but democracy in Iran has and still is rather difficult. To this day, most scholars and international relations experts agree that democratic principles are not honored in Iran, and that individual freedoms, especially those of women and children, are significantly limited as compared to the more liberal countries of the West.

This can be understood more easily when taking a broader look at the development of Iran as a nation. Landholder classes, powerful regional governments, and an absolute monarch have been integral parts of Iranian/Persian culture since halfway through the 1st millennium BCE. And given the course of history under the Qajars—mainly the intrusion of foreign powers into Iranian affairs—it's also not a surprise that the rise of democracy in Iran also coincided with a rise in anti-Western sentiment, which led 20th-century superpowers Britain and the United States to support autocratic Iranian governments instead of a true government by the people.

Additionally, the Qajars presided over Iran during World War I, and although they were officially neutral, they were invaded by the Ottomans shortly after fighting broke out. However, their response was largely defensive, and Iran was able to avoid occupation by their long-time rivals. The Russians would also play a significant role in limiting the Qajar Dynasty's power. Not only did they force them out of the Caucuses, but they also managed to keep Iran from advancing elsewhere to the north or east.

Overall, the Qajar Dynasty, although much less powerful than those that came before it, played a significant role in the development of modern Iran. It helped usher in new eras of more democratic rule, industrialization, and scientific achievement spurred by an investment in public and higher education. Its eventual downfall can be understood as part of a broader trend in which medieval monarchies were replaced by more modern forms of government, but with the Qajar family still alive today, the possibility still exists that the Persian monarchs could once again rise to power and glory.

Conclusion

This brief discussion of the various dynasties that existed after the Achaemenids does not do justice to the glory and splendor Persia has experienced over the past 2,000 years. However, it should help show how this once great empire still lives on today. The forms of government developed by Darius I helped Persian kings control the territory we now call Iran for the better part of 2,500 years.

But perhaps more importantly, the success of these dynasties helped maintain Persian culture and establish a sense of Persian identity, something that is still alive and well today. And the overall policies of religious tolerance and regional autonomy have helped establish Iran as a dynamic, multicultural country that is one of the most powerful and significant in not only the surrounding regions but also in the world.

Chapter 9 – Persian Art: Mixing East and West

The emergence of the Persians at the middle of the last millennium BCE makes them relative newcomers to the western Asian stage. However, once they arrived, they quickly became one of the most formidable powers in the world. While continuous rule of their homeland, the Iranian plateau, escaped them—conquest by the Greeks under Alexander and later the Muslims of Arabia interrupted long periods of Persian rule—the dominance of their empires under the Achaemenid and the Sassanian Dynasties helped establish a strong Persian culture that would persist no matter who controlled Iran.

Because of their ability to remain a strong power throughout much of antiquity and the medieval period, the Persians were able to develop a strong artistic culture that would profoundly influence that of other civilizations.

However, distinguishing which contributions are specifically Persian can sometimes be a tall task. When the Persians arrived on the scene, Mesopotamia had been inhabited for thousands of years, and the Sumerians, Babylonians, and Assyrians had all managed to build large empires that heavily influenced the development of the region. Then, in the 7th century CE, the Persians were conquered by Muslims, pushing their native religion, Zoroastrianism, out of favor, and ushering in the Golden Age of Islam. During this time, the Persians made significant contributions to Muslim art, and Persia itself was considered a hotspot for Muslim cultural development.

As a result, it's best to understand Persian cultural contributions less as true innovations and more as innovative additions. They built on previous cultures and traditions that came from their neighbors, such as the Assyrians, Babylonians, and Medes, but also from those territories that were on the outskirts or even beyond the borders of Persian-controlled lands, such as Greece, Rome, Russia, India, and to a lesser extent, China. However, despite this amalgamation, Persia was able to make its own mark and what came out of the Iranian plateau would help push world culture forward and contributed significantly to its advancement.

Architecture

Much like their contemporaries, Persian kings were obsessed with building. With conquest came great riches, and nearly all the Persian monarchs were concerned with using these riches to help build palaces and other residences that would demonstrate their success as a conqueror and also help them legitimize their claim to the throne.

As a result, much of the artistic achievements of the Persian Empire are found in and around palaces and other royal installations. Art would not have been a more widespread occupation likely until after the Islamic period began in Persia, so skilled artisans would have congregated in the Persian capitals, starting first with Persepolis and then moving toward Susa and Ctesiphon (the capital of the Sassanian Dynasty, which is in present-day Iraq).

The most significant contributions the Persians made in terms of building was their continued development of columns. This is a perfect example of the Persians taking a previously existing form of art or architecture and building upon it to make it their own. And the remaining evidence of this exists in Persepolis, one of the main capitals of the Achaemenid Empire. The columns used there were heavily influenced by the Greeks, who were famous for using columns to support their post and beam construction, but they also incorporated their own style elements. For example, Persian columns have what is known as a Persian animal capital, which refers to the use of animal sculptures as the capital (the top part of a column.) The images below show a classic example of a Persian animal capital column.

Animals show up frequently in ancient Persian architecture, with one of the most notable uses being to "guard" palaces and other important buildings. This was a practice developed originally by the Egyptians, but since the Egyptians were frequently conquered by other empires in the region, this style spread quickly, and nearly all of the important buildings in the key Persian cities of Persepolis and Pasargadae have beautifully sculpted animals standing guard at their entrances.

As time progressed, the Persians began to adapt other styles, most notably that of the Romans. Instead of using post and beam construction techniques, the Romans favored arch-supported buildings, something that would go on to also heavily influence the building styles of most European cultures. The most famous example of this is the Sassanian palace at Ctesiphon, which makes use of engaged columns and blind arches, which are built into the structure instead of outside it, to form a uniquely Persian-Roman style of building. The picture below helps give an idea as to what this style is.

Persian architecture would begin to undergo a transformation after the Muslim invasion. This is why Persian art is usually divided into two periods: pre- and post-Islamic. Post-Islamic Persian architecture incorporated many of the style elements most notable to Islamic art, such as colorful mosaics, large, repeating patterns, calligraphy, stucco, and mirror work. Much of this architecture is on display in the mosques found throughout Iran, as this would have been one of the primary projects of Persian architects, builders, and artisans throughout the Islamic period.

Furthermore, the Persians adapted the Islamic flare for grandeur, choosing to construct large palaces, mosques, parks, and city squares, which would all become defining characteristics of Persian buildings during the Islamic period. Perhaps the best example of this is Naqsh-e Jahan Square, which was built in the 16th century during the time of the Persian Safavid Dynasty. Located in the modern-day city of Isfaha, it's considered to be the sixth-largest city square in the world, and it's a defining piece of post-Islamic Persian architecture. The picture below shows some of the stylistic components of the square's architecture, and it also gives an idea as to just how large this part of the city was.

However, as we should expect, this exchange of artistic styles and techniques was not a one-way street. The Persians themselves, with their rich, vibrant history and culture, managed to make an impact on Islamic architecture, and this is evident throughout the world. Specifically, the Persians were responsible for the inclusion of large-scale domes into Islamic architecture.

This practice was most likely first developed by the Persians under the Sassanian Dynasty, with the most famous buildings being the Palace of Ardashirt and Dezh Dohtar. These domes were relatively new in western Asia and the Near East, but they quickly became a central aspect of nearly all Islamic buildings.

It is for reasons like this why Persia is considered to be one of the driving forces behind the Islamic art culture that dramatically influenced the way the world designed and built buildings. Buildings incorporating these stylistic elements can be found in regions of the world ranging as far as India to Spain. Of course, it would be inaccurate to say Persia was solely responsible for this development, but it would also be inaccurate to say Persian artists and architects did not heavily influence much of the building that took place across western Asia before, during, and after the Islamic Golden Age.

Sculpture and Painting

Persian styles of art and architecture are evident in their buildings, but beyond that, there are many other examples of how Persian art was influenced by and also influenced the artistic development of cultures in the region.

Ancient Persian sculptures came in two forms. The first was sculpted reliefs, which were usually found in temples or palaces. These works are great examples of how Persian art was a true mix between East and West. For example, the Europeans, mostly through the Greeks and Romans, were known for highly-realistic sculptures. They seemed to be most interested in depicting the natural world as accurately and precisely as possible. On the other hand, ancient Mesopotamian cultures favored far more stylized designs, ones that played up the supernatural or even surreal elements of reality.

However, what we see in Persian reliefs is a true mix between these two approaches. For example, consider the relief depicted below. Close attention to detail has been given to the two animals, with the sculptors clearly concerned with trying to be precise in terms of proportions and size. However, the face of the second animal is highly stylized, which helps to show the Persian interest in some of the techniques commonly used in western Asia at the time.

The other significant component of Persian sculpture was its metalwork. The Persians were known for creating quite beautiful statuettes, rhytons (small vessels that can be used as a goblet or a pitcher), and jewelry. Again, these pieces represented a nice mix between Eastern and Western style, which would have made them rather unique and therefore highly desired by citizens across the empire.

These items represent one of the few opportunities for common citizens to enjoy the art created as a result of imperial splendor. Few if any commoners could have afforded sculptures or reliefs in their home, and so owning one of these small, yet finely-crafted trinkets would have been a great source of pride and a family's or individual's chance to express their wealth. As a result, these pieces would have made up a bulk of the luxury trade items the Persians sent to other parts of the empire, making them an important source of wealth for Persian merchants.

Painting

Painting in the Persian Empire did not become common until around the time of the Muslim conquest. Few wall paintings remain from the pre-Islamic period, so it's difficult to tell if this was just not a common practice or if time has simply caused these works to disappear. However, after Muslim conquest and during the time of the post-Islamic dynasties, Persian painting developed significantly and contributed to the overall development of Islamic art.

Perhaps the best-known examples of this are the Persian miniatures. These small paintings were used to accompany storytelling, usually used to depict narrative scenes in the many different books developed in post-Islamic Persia.

Two main stylistic elements stand out from Persian miniatures. The first is that Persian art never fully forbade depiction of the human form, something that was common in many Muslim-controlled territories. This helps demonstrate the relative autonomy Persia was able to maintain during the period of foreign rule from the 8th century CE to the 16th. And while the accuracy of these painters was still not quite up to the same standard as what we would see from the Old Masters that appeared in Europe during the Renaissance, these paintings help to show what people may have looked like, how they dressed, and also how they lived.

The other major contribution that came about from the painting of these miniatures was the concept of "Illumination." This describes the practice of surrounding paintings or even texts with highly-decorative, highly-ornamental designs. The purpose was to try and showcase more beautifully the work of art being presented. Some of the best examples of this are in the copies of the Qur'an that came out of Persia during this time. Because these designs were so successful in beautifying certain texts, many artists began to focus their efforts entirely on these decorative patterns, which helped contribute to perhaps one of Persian's most famous contributions to world art: Persian carpets. The image below depicts a Persian miniature surrounded by a highly-decorative border.

Carpets and Rugs

No discussion of Persian art would be complete without mention of carpets and rugs. The interesting thing about carpet production in Persia, though, is that it was first and foremost a trade. In the ancient world, art was usually something relegated to those who could afford luxury. It was produced by those who were fortunate enough to receive training in the arts, and it was created for those with the wealth, power, and status needed to afford art in the home.

However, in Persia, much like in the rest of the "Rug Belt" (the term used to describe the countries most known for carpet production in the Middle East, ranging from Persia to India), carpet weaving was developed as a means of subsistence by various nomadic tribes; carpets would be designed, created, and brought to market to be sold.

Because of this tradition, it is difficult to pin down any one particular style to describe Persian carpets, but they are in part defined by their exceptional elaborateness and intricate designs, which has helped make them one of the world's most desired commodities.

For example, some designs reflected the nomadic lifestyle of those who made them, telling stories of herding animals and of living on the plains of central Asia, whereas others are clearly designed with an eye for pure aesthetics, using repeated patterns and other intricate design elements most commonly seen in post-Islamic Persia.

Persian carpet weaving likely turned into more of an industry under the Safavids, who built what can be best described as factories in the city of Isfahan (these were more centers of production than full-on, mechanized factories, but the principle is the same). Here the Safavid kings dedicated significant resources to the designs and production of Persian carpets, helping them to become one of the staples of Persian luxury trades. These carpets became so famous that they were desired by the wealthy and powerful from around the world, and many Persian carpets are now on display in museums around the world. Below is a picture of the Ardabil Carpet, housed part of the time in London and part of the time in Los Angeles, and also the Coronation Carpet, which was purchased by the Danish royal family in the 17th century and is kept in Copenhagen.

95

Persian carpet making has been inscribed by UNESCO into their "Intangible Cultural Heritage Lists." Their production represents an important aspect of both the artistic and economic development of the region throughout history. It would have stimulated trade within the empire, and it would have also helped Persia connect with more powerful civilizations in both Europe and Asia. Furthermore, carpet design both benefited from and contributed to the intricate designs used in many other forms of Persian and Islamic art, helping the region develop what would become one of its defining artistic styles.

Conclusion

As we might expect, Persian art is very much a reflection of its history. Persia's emergence onto the stage thousands of years after the Egyptians, Babylonians, and Sumerians had all settled the Fertile Crescent meant that early Persian art heavily reflected the styles of these previous cultures. However, as Persia became more powerful, it began to assert its own influence on the region's art. Eventually, by the time of the Muslim conquest of Persia, it had developed a strong enough artistic culture to not only survive this period of dramatic transformation, but to also influence it in a way that would make Persia an important part of the overall development of Middle Eastern culture.

Chapter 10 – Persian Contributions to Science and Technology

A civilization's ability to produce scientific and technological advancements has a direct impact on its success. The world's most powerful civilizations have all reached their positions as a result of using science to gain an advantage over their adversaries.

Persia is no different. Although their distant neighbors and long-time rivals, the Greeks, with famous names such as Aristotle, Pythagoras, and Archimedes, are responsible for many of the most significant scientific developments of the ancient world, the Persians themselves made many contributions that helped bring human civilization forward and established them as the main power in western Asia.

Ancient Persia

One of the most significant advancements to come out of ancient Persia was the *qanat*. Although there remains some debate as to whether or not the *qanat* was entirely the invention of the Persians—

similar structures appear throughout Mesopotamia and Arabia around the same time—evidence suggests the Persians were able to advance this technology and use it to help them grow into a powerful force. There are more *qanats* in Persia than in any other part of the world

A *qanat* is essentially a system of irrigation. It involves the building of a gently sloping canal through a mountain that taps into the underground water table and provides a steady stream of water for both drinking and irrigation. In many ways, a *qanat* is an underground aqueduct, although constructing this canal underground would have presented the Persians with considerable challenges; the construction of so many of these structures suggests the Persians were significantly advanced at the time. Today, the Qanats of Gonabad are still in use. They are some of the oldest in the world, and they provide water to some 40,000 people living in modern-day Iran. Below is a diagram of how a *qanat* is constructed and how it provides water to the land and people.

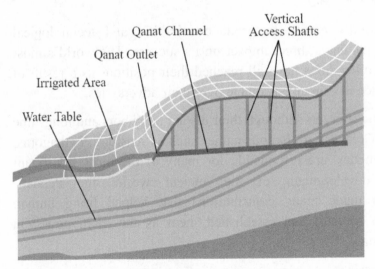

The other major technological development to come out of ancient Persia was the windmill. The Babylonians had developed a windwheel and used it as a pump for irrigation staring in the 18th century BCE, but shortly after the Persians settled the Iranian

plateau, they began using a windmill, which served the same purpose as the Babylonian windwheel but is more effective.

The ancient Persians are also responsible for creating the world's first battery, a device known as the Baghdad Battery. It consisted of a terracotta pot, which was filled with sand, and a large iron rod that was enclosed in a copper tube, which would have been able to conduct electricity. However, a lack of sources describing this device and its heavily corroded state upon discovery have made it hard for historians to determine with any accuracy what exactly this device would have been used for. Some theories suggest it was used as a galvanic cell, or as a tool for electroplating, or a method of electrotherapy. Nonetheless, the Baghdad Battery dates to the time near the end of the Parthian and beginning of the Sassanian dynasties, suggesting the Persians at the time were leaders in science and technology.

Islamic and Post-Islamic Persia

After the Muslim conquest of Persia, the ancient power continued to contribute to the development of modern science. One of the more notable contributions was the 11th-century philosopher, Biruni, wrote in an astronomical text that the earth might rotate around the sun. At the time, cultures around the world believed in a geocentric universe, meaning the Earth was at its center. And although Biruni had no material evidence to support this claim, we can look back on his statement and attribute it to the great scientific culture that existed in Persia at the time.

The Law of the Conservation of Mass, which was proved by Lomonosov and Laurent Lavoisier in the 18th century and states that a body of matter never disappears but rather just changes from one form to another, also has its origins in Persia, with the philosopher Tusi first writing this idea down. Tusi also wrote down some of the world's first inquiries into the concept of evolution, but he was doing so in an attempt to make a religious argument, and therefore cannot be given too much credit for this discovery.

Another important scientist of the Islamic period, Jaber Ibn Hayyan, is considered to be one of the founding fathers of modern chemistry. He published an encyclopedia that outlined his thoughts on subjects such as the applications of tanning and textiles, the distillation of plants and flowers, the origin of perfumes, and how gunpowder could be used . Perhaps this last topic was what had such a lasting influence on world history, for the East discovered and made use of gunpowder long before the West, and its discovery led to the formation of the Gunpowder Empires, which used this technology to establish firm control over territory in western and central Asia.

Kamal al-Din Al-Farisi was another famous scientist to come out of the Islamic period. He focused more on trying to describe the physical world, and he is credited with coming up with the first legitimate explanation for why a rainbow occurs. However, perhaps more importantly, he made this claim by first presenting a theory and then running rigorous experiments to verify it, suggesting he may have helped usher in the use of the scientific method and rationalism into Iran, which would become driving forces of scientific development throughout the medieval period and beyond.

The other area where the Persians helped make significant advancements in science was in medicine. It's believed the Achaemenid Persians invented the concept of organ transplants, although little evidence exists to suggest they were able to do these procedures reliably and successfully.

One of the most popular things to look at in the development of Persian medicine is the way in which they diagnosed and then treated headaches. For much of history, this common ailment was not understood, yet Persian doctors set out to try and figure out what caused these headaches and how they could be cured. They made detailed observations of the different types of headaches, classifying them by the symptoms they produced and their potential causes.

This culture of observation and experimentation helped Persia develop into a center for medicine in the medieval world, a culture that has continued until the present day. The founding of the Academy of Gundishapur under the Sassanian Dynasty in the 6th century CE represents the world's first teaching hospital. People from all over the world, from Greece to India, would come to Gundishapur to study and practice, taking what they learned back with them to their home. This academy is still around today and is considered one of the world's premier medical schools.

In the field of mathematics, the Persians made many accomplishments, especially while under Islamic rule, which dedicated significant resources to the development of mathematics. Perhaps one of the most significant things to come out of Persian math, though, was the 10th century CE invention of the logarithm table by Muhammad Ibn Musa-al-Kharazmi. He also made significant contributions to the development of algebra, and he also expanded upon both Persian and Indian arithmetic. Because of all of his work, al-Kharazmi is considered to be one of the fathers of modern mathematics.

Conclusion

The Persians established themselves as a distinct cultural and linguistic group over 2,000 years ago. And given their success at establishing and holding an empire throughout that time, it should come as no surprise that the Persians were able to make significant contributions to the development of world culture. However, their achievements in science and technology are among some of the most important. Today, the modern-day nation of Iran continues to be a high achiever in the world of science. Important international conferences are held each year throughout the country, and Iran continues to be a leader in modern medicine, helping to continue the legacy and splendor of the Persian Empire into the modern era.

Conclusion

As the crossroads between Europe and Asia, the Middle East has played a critical role in the development of the world we live in today. The many different imperial powers that emerged from this region—known by many as the Cradle of Civilization—helped to draw the borders of some of the world's most powerful and populous countries. And at the center of all of this was Persia.

Unlike the Assyrians or the Babylonians, once the Persians entered the scene in western Asia in the 7th century BCE, they became central components to the region's social, political, and cultural development. Not only did the Persian Empire lay the groundwork for a common Persian culture and identity, but it helped establish the borders of the modern-day nation of Iran, helped spread Islam throughout the Middle East, and taught the world how to effectively and efficiently administer a vast empire.

The first Persian Empire—the Achaemenid Empire—controlled all of western Asia as well as parts of Africa and even Europe. And while subsequent dynasties would be unable to match the territorial achievements of the Achaemenids, they would help to establish the Iranian people and their country as an economic power that would be critical in helping to establish East-West trade and diplomatic relations.

Today, Persia, or Iran, is in a time of political uncertainty. The Iranian Revolution of 1977 brought democracy to the country, building off the constitutional reforms that were carried out at the beginning of the 20th century, but this did not bring stability. Its Supreme Leader has become rather powerful, and in the face of international antagonism, it has fallen slightly out of favor on the world stage.

However, the history of Persia shows us one thing: this culturally-distinct, proud, and advanced society is here to stay. Time and time again, defeat or instability has threatened Persia, but it always found a way to reassert itself as a dominant force in the region, and there is every reason to believe this will continue to be the case, especially when considering Iran holds the largest reserves of natural gas, the fossil fuel that is quickly becoming the world's favorite.

Overall, there's no telling what the Persia of tomorrow will look like, but if its past is any indication, then it's safe to assume it will be an important country capable of shaping not only the course of Middle Eastern history but of the entire world.

Bibliography

Amanat, Abbas. *Pivot of the Universe: Nasir al-Din Shah Qajar and the Iranian Monarchy, 1831-1896*. Univ of California Press, 1997.

Bower, Virginia, et al. *Decorative Arts, Part II: Far Eastern Ceramics and Paintings, Persian and Indian Rugs and Carpets*. National Gallery of Art, Washington, 1998

Bury, J.B; Cook, S.A.; Adcock, F.E. *The Persian Empire and the West* in: The Cambridge Ancient History Vol. IV. Cambridge University Press, 1930

Fisher, William Bayne; Avery, P.; Hambly, G. R. G; Melville, C. *The Cambridge   History of Iran*. Cambridge University Press.

Frye, Richard N. *The Sassanians*. Cambridge Ancient History Vol. 122 . Cambridge Univesity Press, 2005.

Kuhrt, Amélie. *The Persian Empire: A Corpus of Sources from the Achaemenid Period*. Routledge, 2013.

Nicolle, David; McBride, Angus. *Sassanian Armies: The Iranian Empire Early 3rd to mid-7th centuries AD*. Montvert Publications, 1996.

Olmstead, Albert Ten Eyck. *History of the Persian Empire. Vol. 108.* Chicago: University of Chicago Press, 1948.

Wiesehofer, Josef. *Ancient Persia.* IB Tauris, 2001.

Made in United States
North Haven, CT
12 January 2022

14477637R00071